The Illusion of Beauty: Why Women Hate Themselves & Envy Other Women

THE ILLUSION OF BEAUTY: WHY WOMEN HATE THEMSELVES & ENVY OTHER WOMEN

Cassandra A. George Sturges, MA, MA Psy.D

iUniverse, Inc.

New York Lincoln Shanghai

The Illusion of Beauty: Why Women Hate Themselves & Envy Other Women

iUniverse books may be ordered through booksellers or by contacting:

iUniverse
2021 Pine Lake Road, Suite 100
Lincoln, NE 68512
www.iuniverse.com
1-800-Authors (1-800-288-4677)

Because of the dynamic nature of the Internet, any Web addresses or links contained in this book may have changed since publication and may no longer be valid.

The views expressed in this work are solely those of the author and do not necessarily reflect the views of the publisher, and the publisher hereby disclaims any responsibility for them.

ISBN: 978-0-595-46022-9 (pbk)
ISBN: 978-0-595-90323-8 (ebk)

Printed in the United States of America

To the two women who rule my heart: my mother, Mary & my daughter, Amanda

Contact Author:

Authentik Beauty
P.O. Box 980679
Ypsilanti, Michigan 48197
Http://Authentikbeauty.blogspot.com
WWW.AuthentikBeauty.net
Authentikbeauty@yahoo.com

CONTENTS

CHAPTER 1

▼

THE POWER OF BEAUTY

Why Women Hate Other Women

Women instinctively know that men have little power when it comes to sexual intercourse in male and female relationships. Women know that if a platonic relationship exists between a male and a female, ninety percent of the time it is a platonic relationship because the woman does not want to have sex with the man instead of visa versa. Most women do not feel that men are psychologically or biologically capable of resisting another woman's sexual prowess because of their undying love, loyalty and respect for their committed relationship with them. If a man does not engage in a sexual relationship with a woman who is drop-dead gorgeous, most women believe that it is because the other woman was in control of the outcome and whether or not it is a sexual or non-sexual relationship. Women intuitively know that most heterosexual males find extraordinarily beautiful women sexually irresistible and if that extraordinarily beautiful woman wanted her man, he would be hers for the taking.

Have you ever watched a man try not to look at a beautiful woman in the presence of his female companion? He is desperately nervous as he attempts to look at his shoes, but there appears to be a biological magnetic pull that forces him to visually consume this woman's beauty, if only in his imagination. And though most women pretend not to notice or feel threatened by his behavior, most of us feel intimidated and small inside. We feel insecure and easily replaceable. We notice how physically attractive this woman is and painfully compare ourselves to her. This subject is too taboo to talk about, but these are the seeds that sprout low self-esteem; the competition between women, constant dieting and the need to be noticed by other men.

As a woman, I have encountered many men who supposedly love the woman with whom they are in a monogamous relationship, but literally beg me for a kiss, a date, my telephone number and/or sex. Every woman reading this book knows that the reason that so many men remain faithful to their female partners is because we turned them down. We sent him home. We told him, "No, you can't have this!" We know inside that if we wanted to, we could rock another woman's world and steal her man … if we felt like it. We also know that we are just as vulnerable to another woman doing the same thing to us. We secretly wonder if other women will be kind enough to send our man home to us.

How many times have you observed a man coupled with a woman but who could not keep his eyes off of you? A part of you was disgusted and judged that man as being a scum of the earth, but another part of you felt flattered because you conquered your enemy … the other woman. You made her man look at you, in a manner that was only meant for her. You made her man want you. He can't keep his eyes off of you, but yet he is supposed to love her. Although women call men dogs, and accuse them of being sexually unfaithful in a monogamous relationship; they know that it was another woman who led him to the dog house.

Many women get angry when I bring up this topic. But so many women are in denial about how cutthroat and backstabbing women are to other women. Women talk about how disrespectful men are to them when they make derogatory sexual comments about their body parts. However the reason we as women dress provocatively in the first place is because we want to entice and attract men. Women would be absolutely insulted if they had exposed their cleavage, belly, thong and the crevice of our buttocks and no one noticed. Women dress sexy, sleazy, cheap, and slutty and then have the audacity to get angry at men for noticing. This is insane. Women say that they dress for themselves; they want to feel good about their bodies. This is true to a certain degree. But when you wash your car in your front yard, in a too, small, bikini on a Sunday afternoon; at a subconscious level, you know in your spirit that you are doing this to tantalize the men and annoy their wives. We know how to wear clothes that conceal, yet are stylish and 'classy'. Now, please note, I absolutely don't have a problem with women dressing provocatively, I am only saying to women, please stop pretending that you don't know what you are doing. Stop pretending that you are annoyed at a man for noticing the tightest jeans that you could fit your ass into. Stop pretending that you are offended that a man is staring at your naked cleavage that you purposely exposed. As women we need to be honest with ourselves about our true intentions and motivations and how we use the sexual power of femininity and beauty to intimidate, erode and destroy the self-esteem of other women.

I find it amusing when a woman to tells me, as she takes a sip from her fifth glass of vodka and a long drag from the last cigarette in the pack, that the reason that she is constantly dieting is because she wants to be healthy.

Why does a man need to look at other women in a sexual manner when he is supposed to be in love with you? When a man is looking at another woman's nude body, isn't he imagining what it would be like to touch her? While we may feel insecure about our stretch marks, sagging breasts, big stomach, cellulite and flabby thighs, we feel that if we were beautiful enough he would never want to look at another woman's nude body in a sexual way.

Not only are women's bodies compared to other women in one-on-one intimate relationships,; but women are, directly and indirectly, constantly compared at a societal level to the physical attractiveness of other women. They don't feel that they will ever be perfect enough to be loved and accepted unconditionally for who they are. Men don't wear clothes to show the size of their penis. But women are constantly judged by the shape of their ass and the size of their breasts. The only thing that separates a woman from other women in her man's life is the sexual intimacy; otherwise her relationship is no different from the one that he shares with his secretary, mother, sister, neighbor and friend.

Why do women hate other women?

1. A woman feels that her biological prime-time is limited. She can easily be replaced by a new, younger, more beautiful woman. Youth is a woman's fair-weather friend.

2. A woman feels that other women control their man's sexual fidelity.

3. A woman feels that her level or degree of physical beauty is based on luck as opposed to something that she controls.

4. A woman feels that other women can take something that they have worked hard to earn by using their beauty on the job, school and the legal system because men will be taken by her beauty.

5. Women feel that other women cannot be trusted. They gossip too much, they are phony and they would take your man right before your eyes.

6. A woman feels that other women divert attention away from them.

7. A woman psychologically feels competitive with other women to be more attractive.

8. A woman subconsciously believes that if she merely looked like that other woman, she could inherit her life, her diamonds, her man, and that people would look at her with the same admiration.

Male Identity

Men were born into this world to create their own unique identity through their actions and deeds. When society tells little boys to "be a man," there is no script, divine plan or biological clock that guides their destiny. A healthy male can father a child at the age of 19, 39 or 99. Biologically, males never stop reproducing … thus never shedding any aspects of their male identity as they ages. Through biological design nature has given males the freedom to discover, create, and shape their role and identity in society. They can choose from a variety of careers, activities and hobbies that uniquely define masculinity for them. Little boys evolve into men and men create their own destiny.

Males always have an opportunity to "be somebody" as long as there is breath in his body. All a man needs to do to redeem himself and to increase his value in society is to come up with a great idea, a side-splitting joke, a new song, a better light bulb, a new method of transportation or a more efficient weapon. His worthiness to society is not attached to his muscle mass, rippled abdominals, chiseled cheek bones, or broad shoulders. Nature has given him the freedom to build and shape his environment to make up for any physical shortcoming that he may imagine himself to have. Since he could not kill a lion with his bare hands man invented and constructed weapons that vouchsafed him mastery. Man could not see in the dark, so he created means of lighting up the darkness. When man grew tired of the limitations of walking he rode horses and camels and later designed the car. Man could not swim across the ocean so he built boats and later ships.

Man could not fly like the birds but he ultimately designed an airplane. Instead of using his psychological energy to curse nature for not bestowing on him stronger muscles, better eyes, faster legs or wings, he decided to reorder the world to adapt to his needs. Men do not focus on their flaws, their imperfections or what they lack; instead they use what nature has given them to make the world into a better place for them. Men create their own purpose; not satisfied with the limitations of nature, nor of their own bodies … but instead, using their intellect, imagination and soul, to reorder things according to their desires.

Through personal accomplishments, men compensate for their short stature, bald head, big belly and small penis by manipulating the physical universe through technology, science, medicine and architecture. A rich, intelligent, and powerful man will always be able to select from a bevy of beauties whether or not he is physically attractive as Denzel Washington and Brad Pitt. However, Queen Elizabeth, Janet Reno and Condoleezza Rice with all of their wealth, wisdom and power combined will have difficulty magnetizing attractive males to share their beds to engage in mad, passionate sex. Unfortunately, in today's society a man's greatest asset is his mind and a woman's greatest asset is her behind.

We tell little boys what they should not do, how they should not act and how they should not feel. We tell male children that little boys don't cry; boys don't show their emotions; and boys aren't afraid of danger. Boys are usually told who and what they are not, but never who they are, or who they should be, or how they should behave. Men have the psychological and societal freedom to define themselves for themselves. This is the root and essence of confidence and self-esteem.

Female Identity

From the time that little girls are born, society expects them to fit into a certain mold, a particular role and possess certain characteristics. The characteristics that are expected of them are assumed to be natural and inflexible. Little girls are always instructed on how they should look, how they should behave and how they should feel. Little girls should be beautiful, dainty, neat, polite, nurturing and well behaved. When she deviates from the identity given to her by society she becomes disillusioned about her self-worth and role in society. This is the root and essence of what eliminates confidence and is the basis of self-hatred and low self-esteem.

Women are born in to a world that has a pre-established female identity, purpose, role and destiny that includes the time constraints of a biological clock. If a woman never develops a career, gets a job, writes a book, conducts research or creates new technology or inventions … most likely society will never say to her, "be a woman." She was born a woman. If she is born an extraordinary, beautiful, attractive woman the world will be given to her without her ever having to ask. She will walk into a room and own it. Her mere appearance could stop traffic. Men will declare love and admiration for her, simply because her appearance is pleasing to the eye. Women will envy and fear her.

Nature's genetic blueprint bestows women with their most valued assets that are sought after in a patriarchal society. Nature's own, home grown, breasts, nails, long silken hair, beautiful face, flat stomach, round-shapely buttocks and firms thighs are better than any man-created, artificial body enhancements. The artificial, lab-created beauty is acceptable but is not as powerful and admired as the real thing. One of my friends called me at work and stated that it was an emergency. My friend's voice was filled with sheer joy and enthusiasm. My immediate thought was that she had gotten the job promotion that she wanted. She told me over the phone to sit down before she could share her good news with me. I sat down as I held the telephone to my ear as my heart pounded. "Okay," I said. "What happened?" She exclaimed through the phone, "Girl, did you know that Beyonce's hair is not really that long. I saw a picture of her at an airport and my hair is longer than that bitch's. Can you believe it!? She ain't all that."

Can you imagine a man calling another man to tell him, that John is wearing a toupee with the same enthusiasm? Women compete with other women from the outside in. They gauge their self-worth based on how they measure up to other women, not their own standards of success and beauty. It's okay for them to be 160 pounds, as long as the woman next door is 170 pounds. When one woman goes on a diet, many times her associates and friends will follow suit. Not because they really feel like they need to go on a diet, but because they do not want their friend to be smaller or perceived as being more physically attractive.

What most women fail to realize is that: No one can be a better you … than you. Let me repeat this again: No one can be a better you … than you. Even if you have a genetic twin, you still have your own unique personality. You are an original, a one and only, a designer human, a creation of God and nature. When you were born your genetic mold was broken. There is absolutely no one else in the world just like you. When you focus on being your truest and most authentic self, there is absolutely no competition in this world. Competition can only exist by psychologically comparing two objects. Why would any person's opinion about you be more potent, powerful and important than your own? Why do you feel that you should have been born with a different face, body or eye color? Why should any person love, respect and cherish you more than you do yourself?

Many women imitate Marilyn Monroe's femme fatale persona, but none of them are remembered and celebrated like her. Marilyn Monroe's image is still imitated by modern performers such as Madonna and Christina Aguilera. A butterfly could never be a magnificent hummingbird, but when it accepts its divine genetic design; its beauty is beyond comparison.

Most women don't feel like they have the power to create and value their own identity. Women do not have the opportunity to select or create "societal expectations and standards" of the ideal female identity. Nor do women have the opportunity to say, "Hey, God, when I go to earth as a woman, I want a physical appearance that will allow me to feel loved and accepted by society. I want blond hair; mesmerizing violet blue eyes, double D firm breasts, a 32 inch waistline and 36 inch hips. I want my lips to be full and to have a beguiling pout and I would like to be equipped with a small upturned nose. Oh yeah, I want to be able to eat normal meals and have beautiful babies without stretch marks and sagging breasts. And as a bonus, I want a husband who will never look at another woman in lust. That's all!"

Women hate other women because they feel that the gods, goddesses, nature, and/or the universe has randomly and unjustly distributed women's most desired physical assets to only a few lucky women. From a societal perspective, women cannot make up for with good deeds, advances in technology and creative designs to compensate for nature's lack of generosity. Women inherit the bodies that they are born in and they make do. They can enhance, tuck, and tip what nature has given them, but the closer they are born into looking like the ideal female beauty the easier their lives will be. A knight can become a king, but can a woman who severely deviates from the modern standards of beauty ever become a beauty queen? Women know in the depths of their souls and the bowels of their guts, that true mesmerizing, captivating, intoxicating, irresistible physical beauty can never be substituted, created, designed or imitated by other human beings. This is why the Cinderella fairytale is so significant in American culture. Cinderella's stepsisters and stepmother could not compete with her beauty in order to win the prince.

The stepsisters and stepmother could purchase shoes, clothes and cosmetics to enhance their appearance; but obtaining these items would still not be enough to win over the prince because they did not possess natural beauty. Society sets the cultural standards for what is to be considered beautiful. Based on these societal standards, if you are a woman … you are either born with true beauty, or born trying to get it. This is one of the root causes of why women hate themselves and other women. Superficially and generally speaking, in a capitalistic society, a woman's appearance is more valuable than her intellectual, academic and athletic accomplishments.

The Power of Beauty

Attractive people have advantages in our society that supersede wealth, class, race, prestige and gender. Research studies indicate that:

- We believe in the stereotype that what is beautiful is good. We believe that physically attractive people possess other desirable characteristics such as intelligence, competence, social skills, confidence and moral character. Children's fairy tales make a point of saying that the good princess is beautiful and the bad witch, stepmother, stepsisters, etc are ugly.

- In all social situations people respond more positively to physically attractive people. Teachers who are attractive receive higher student evaluations from their students. Students who are attractive receive more attention and help from their teachers.

- Even with people who share the exact same level of education, experience and credentials, the more physically attractive candidate is more likely to be offered the job. Attractive applicants have a better chance of getting jobs, and of receiving higher salaries.

- Attractive people are more popular in school, the work place and social clubs.

- In court, attractive people are found guilty less often. When found guilty, they receive less severe sentences.

- One study found that there was a direct relationship between the size and number of diamond carats in a woman's engagement ring based on her degree of physical attractiveness. The bigger the diamond, the more attractive is the woman.

- People who are attractive have more choices in selecting romantic partners and thus have more power in the relationship.

- Attractive people are more likely to marry into wealthy families. One study found that the more attractive a woman is, the higher the level of her husband's education.

- A study by Robert Cialdini (1984) he proposes that physically attractive people have an enormous social advantage in our culture; they are better liked, more persuasive, more frequently helped, and seen as possessing better personality traits and intellectual capabilities.

Youth is beauty's only friend. A woman cannot physically give birth to a baby from age 19 to 99; she has a biological prime-time that she must utilize appropriately in order to maximize her future options. She is more likely to attract a wealthy male if she is youthful and fertile. By no means is it written that a woman must become a mother because she has a uterus, but if motherhood is an option that she selects, she must schedule and coordinate it with her other dreams, goals and ambitions. Women can't play competitive tennis while being 7 months pregnant. Women have limited choices in selecting jobs that will accommodate pregnancy and motherhood. Women don't need to nurse their babies anymore they can use bottles. Women don't have to worry about an unplanned pregnancy due to a myriad of birth control methods. But as of this writing in April 2006, women still carry the unborn child. A woman cannot ignore the biological time frame and structure that limits her options as she ages.

Another major factor that impacts women's obsession with their physical appearance is that from a strictly biological standpoint men sexually respond to visual stimuli that are aesthetically appealing. Women are capable of having intercourse whether or not they are physically attracted to their male partner. They can buy a vaginal lubricant to aid in intercourse. Women don't need to have an orgasm in order to become impregnated. The perpetuation of human life does not need women to ever have an orgasm, enjoy sex, or be physically attracted to their male partner in order to conceive. When a man is visually turned on by a woman's physical appearance this helps perpetuate the human species from a biological perspective. Women are desperately trying to look attractive enough to cause the male penis to rise and fall at her command, and in the process she feels that she is in direct competition with other women who may do a superior job.

I believe that there is a biological root to modern day women's obsession with body image that contributes to low self-esteem. Sociologist William Ogburn (1922, 1964) coined the term cultural lag to describe the imbalance between technological advances (material culture ... objects that are tangible, that we can touch) in society with the norms, values and traditional beliefs in a particular society (non-material culture intangible things such as morals, ethics and how we feel about something). Simply stated, we first create the material object before we create the rules on how we will manipulate or use the object that is ethically fair to society in general. For example, we created the car before traffic laws, driver's license and age limits. Scientists created birth control methods that conflict with some religious beliefs and traditional family values. When scientists developed birth control, they probably were not contemplating the pro life and pro choice debate. When humans first create material objects such as the Internet, weapons of mass destruction and cosmetic surgery most likely they do not or cannot take into consideration how these material and technological advances will impact the values, norms, morals and beliefs that lag behind their material inventions.

So what inventions have we created that have changed how women perceive themselves? How can we live in a society where food is readily available and women starve themselves? What could be a rational, logical reason for tolerating hunger pangs in the presence of food? How is it possible for a person to eat their food and purposely vomit to rid themselves of calories? Why would a woman go through the trouble of letting a doctor cut open her breasts to implant foreign objects that do *not* improve her ability to breathe? Why would a woman inject a chemical into her lips to cause them to swell or allow doctors to apply liposuction to her thighs with a vacuum? You guessed it! Advances in technology, and in particular the rise of the mass media have caused normal concerns about how we look to become obsessions. We see the body parts of other people that were, once in the past, private in more and more revealing and seductive media pictorials. We can no longer hide in the family photo albums, tucked away at grandma's house. In addition to cameras and camcorders our cell phones now take pictures of us and project them onto the internet. Everywhere we go, we see ourselves.

Pornographic material is different from seeing other nude bodies in the shower or on the beach. The nude bodies in the magazines are airbrushed. The birthmarks and stretch marks have been erased and the cellulite has been deleted. Even the women themselves cannot compete with their own images in the magazines. Studies show that men who frequently review pornographic material are less sexually attracted to their female partners. Given that men sexually respond best to visual stimuli, If the women in the pornographic magazines have flawless, perfect bodies; is it not possible for him to look at his human, un-brushed, un-enhanced, flesh and blood female partner and not be as aroused by her physical appearance? Do men in committed relationships look at nude pictures of other women and fantasize about having sex with them? Of course they do. Do you think that men compare and contrast their female body parts to the women in the magazines? Of course they do. Men are biologically designed to be attracted to visual stimuli. A woman wants to be the vision of loveliness that her man responds to exclusively. We want to be his one and only favorite eye candy.

Advances in technology that affect the importance of viewed images include television, the Internet, cell phones that take pictures, digital cameras and all types of print media including billboards. Imagine standing in line at the grocery store and while waiting you notice the bikini clad models and celebrities on the cover of the magazines on the racks next to the check out line. How does this make you feel inside? Does it makes you want to suck in your stomach and take the snacks out of your grocery basket? No one directly told you that you were fat or needed to do sit ups or go on a diet; but just viewing those images slowly chips away at your self-esteem. We see models and celebrities more than we see our family and friends. Each time we drive to work we see perfection on the billboards; we see perfection on the television and on the pop-up ads on the Internet. People who look like us are not referred to as gorgeous or beautiful. Because we see celebrities and models all the time they become "real" to us; we then believe that we can attain their extraordinary physique and good looks with self-discipline. We begin to think that if we looked more desirable, our lives would be filled with more love and wealth.

The clincher is that the standards of beauty have been set by technology and computers. The current media ideal of beauty, thinness and physical attractiveness is achievable by less than 3% of the female population. When artists airbrush and digitally enhanced photographs, they never think that real women will want to emulate this illusion of perfection.

The Illusion of Beauty

Why do we women desperately adorn themselves for men to look at them? What is so special about a "look"? Why does a woman become angry, hurt and insecure when the man they love "looks" at another woman in a manner of awe or appreciation of that woman's beauty? Do we as women feel in our hearts that one day the man that we love, will "look" at the physical beauty of another woman and leave us? Can I be the first to say, "I do." As of this writing, I am in a nine-year-relationship with a man who said that the first time he "looked" at me, my beauty, literally took his breath away and he gasped with awe. He described to me what I was wearing and shared many of his journal entries about how much he cared for me. I could have been a child-molesting, serial killer but my physical appearance created an emotional relationship with him that caused him to pursue a really intimate relationship with me. Is it not possible for some other, younger, more beautiful woman to take him away from me, simply because she is beautiful? Of course it takes a lot more than beauty to remain in a long-term relationship, but the thought of him "looking" at another woman causes me to shiver with insecurity.

Women know that the first step in forming a relationship with a male is to entice him to look at us in a desirous, sexual way. Once he is visually interested in our physical appearance, we have set the ground work in order for him to get to know who we are at a much deeper level. And though we hear the saying all of our lives that "Beauty is only skin deep," we know that women who are physically attractive do not need to be "deep" in order for men to pursue them. The image that we project with our clothing, make-up and hairstyle is just an illusion of who we really are on the inside. Underneath the foundation, lipstick, eyeliner, faux lashes, mascara, eye-shadow, hair-weave, gel, nail polish, push-up bra, clothes, shoes and jewelry is the real person.

When women dress up to entice men to look at them, they only want certain men to notice and compliment their beauty. The quality of our beauty image should theoretically attract the quality of the man. A quality male should be wealthy and successful. Have you ever been insulted by a man who requested your phone number or asked you for a date because you felt that, "you looked too damn good for him to have the nerve to come on to you?" Have you or someone you know ever said, "She look too good for him." What we are really saying is that based on her physical appearance she should be able to catch a man who is wealthy and professionally successful. No one ever makes comments about Play-boy bunnies being too young or beautiful for Hugh Hefner. When a man is wealthy, people assume that he is worthy of a young, beautiful attractive woman. When we say that a man "looks" too good for a women, what we are really saying is that not only is he physically more attractive than she is, but he is financially capable of obtaining a much more attractive mate. This man may be looked upon by other women as "snatch material" meaning that those women feel superior and more physically attractive than the woman whom he is with. Therefore, some women may feel that they could take this man away from his comparatively unattractive female partner—if they wanted to. The assumption is that the man "settled" for less than what he is actually worth or deserves because of his level of wealth and physical attractiveness. The resources that men need to attract women increase in value over time. Resources are such things as money, property, pres-tige, as well as physical appeal, as he becomes more distinguished, sexy and attrac-tive. On the other hand, the resources that women need to remain marketable decrease over time; youthful beauty, alluring breasts, sexy buttocks, elastic skin and fertility.

Some of the most celebrated and beautiful women could not control their male partner from "looking" at, and having sexual relationships with, other women. You will never be beautiful enough to stop your man from sexually desir-ing other women. You will never be beautiful enough or perfect enough to stop your man from looking at other women. You will never be perfect enough to stop your man from being aroused by other women. You will never be perfect enough to stop your man from sexually desiring other women. No matter how much weight you lose, plastic surgery you have or Botox you have injected to fill the wrinkles in every crease and crevice of your body and soul—doing these things will never make a man love you or stop him from leaving you; if leaving you is something that he wants to do. Love has no rhyme or reason, no time or season. It just is. It is unconditional, raw, honest, vulnerable and authentic. You don't capture love, love captures you.

CHAPTER 2

▼

UNVEILING THE ILLUSION OF BEAUTY

Why do we as women go through so much pain in order for men to look at us? I think that it is because we simply want to be unconditionally loved. We want our man to love and desire only us. We feel that if we are perfect enough we will then be worthy enough to attract and keep true love. However, the real situation is somewhat different.

The Alpha Male

Who are alpha males? Hugh Hefner, Donald Trump, Michael Jordan famous wealthy athletes, movie stars. Show me a man who is wealthy and famous, and I'll show you a man who is 99.9% likely to be unfaithful in a committed relationship. The alpha male is the individual in the community to whom others defer and follow. Humans and their nearest species-relatives, the chimpanzees, show deference to the alpha of the community by ritualized gestures such as bowing, allowing the alpha to walk first in a procession, or standing aside when the alpha challenges. Canines also show deference to the alpha pair in their pack, by allowing them to be the first to eat and, usually, the only pair to mate. The status of alpha is generally achieved by means of superior physical prowess. Listed below are some of the characteristics of the human alpha male.

- When a man is extraordinary wealthy it doesn't matter how physically unattractive he is because his wealth is a babe-magnet.

- Women will always throw themselves at men who are wealthy, successful, or famous, in order to improve their standard of living.

- Most alpha males, even when they are in committed relationships, will seek sexual intimacy outside of the committed relationship.

- Most alpha males have difficulty interconnecting sex, love and loyalty into one package.

- Alpha males generally believe that they deserve to have more than one woman.

- Alpha males not only collect expensive cars, guns, cigars and antiques, their collection also includes sexual relationships with beautiful women.

- Having a bevy of beautiful women is encouraged and expected behavior of wealthy successful men.

Alpha males need Barbie Dolls in order to maintain their ultra-masculine-male dominant status in society. Barbie Dolls have the ultra-female characteristics that complement his superior alpha status.

Barbie Doll Characteristics include:

- Barbie dolls are plastic. At all costs they must spend money on cosmetic surgery to maintain their youthful appearance. Implants, liposuction, rhinoplasty, breasts lifts, cellulite removal, botox injections, chemical peels and other techniques to maintain or obtain outer appearances, are necessary in order to compete for his affection and attention.

- Barbie dolls do not talk. Alpha men need a woman who is not going to complain about his long work hours, time that he spends with his "boys," his relationship with other women and his lack of participation in domestic matters.

- Barbie dolls smile all the time. The alpha male needs a woman who doesn't reveal her feelings of unhappiness in the relationship. She is going to continue to smile when she learns that he has conceived a child outside of the committed relationship.

- Barbie dolls can be placed on the shelf when the alpha male is finished playing with them. When he falls in love with a younger, hipper, new model with fuller lips, he doesn't have to worry about the long-term affects of the breaking of her heart.

- Barbie dolls need and seek material accessories. The alpha male knows that as long as he is willing to buy her big, fancy homes, expensive cars and jewelry; he doesn't have to worry about being faithful and loyal to the relationship. Barbie dolls need a lot of expensive monetary upkeep. The alpha male has the money to give her whatever she needs because it validates his wealth and prestige.

- Barbie dolls can travel or move at a moment's notice. She has a travel case that comes with her, because she does *not* have a career or goals that cannot be sacrificed or thwarted for an alpha male. She changes locations based on the needs of the alpha male.

- Barbie dolls are always perfect and gorgeous, even naked. Alpha males need trophy wives and arm pieces to accompany them to fancy events. Dieting, exercising and maintaining an impeccable physical appearance are essential to remain attractive to the Alpha male. Due to the competition and availability of other dolls the Barbie doll's desirability is based on her ability to keep the alpha male sexually interested and satisfied.

- The Barbie doll's youth and unchanging beauty is her greatest asset. She has a short shelf life. She must have as many children as quickly as possible to ensure her financial future in old age when she is no longer attractive or able to reproduce.

- Barbie dolls don't ask questions. She is not going to question the alpha male about their future together, his assets or his Swedish bank accounts. She doesn't question pre-nuptial agreements because she knows that her time is limited in the relationship as she will not be able to compete with the newer models and editions that are marketed each year.

- Barbie dolls are hollow on the inside because they must have extremely low-self esteem in order to put up with the Alpha male's malarkey. The alpha male's presence in her life validates her external existence. She believes that her external, physical appearance is the depth of who she is.

Faded Beauty Syndrome

Have you ever noticed a woman who looks all of fifty-five, but is trying to look and act as if she is twenty-five? A fading beauty is a woman who feels, and projects in her behaviors, that her best years are behind her. Her self-esteem and self-worth is based on her physical appearance and how she compares to other women. A fading beauty desperately holds on to her youthful beauty fearing that without it she is invisible. These are precisely the signs of a fading beauty.

As for a faded beauty, the signs are manifold. This is how it feels and plays out.

- In high school, college or during your general youth you were considered to be the most beautiful, the hottest girl around. The guys adored you and you could have any man that you wanted. Now that you have married and/or had children you feel frumpy, old and unattractive. Without your looks, you have no idea of who you are and where you belong in life. You spend most of your time thinking about how you used to look, back in your heyday.

- You haven't changed your hairstyle, makeup, or style of clothes since you were seventeen-years-old. You psychologically compare yourself to younger women thinking to yourself how you could take their man if you were 10 years younger.

- Maybe you wear heavy make-up to hide the bags under your eyes, the wrinkles and age spots on your face. You may feel that without your make up you are unattractive, even when going for a walk or a quick run to the grocery store or gas station.

- Your focus is completely on how you hate your appearance, and on how you might improve it.

- You haven't learned anything new in the last ten years. You don't read books, you haven't taken any classes, and you don't volunteer your time. You are bored with your own life.

- If you talk to someone who has not spoken to you in 10 years, what new things would you tell them about your life? If you have nothing new to talk about you are a faded beauty; not because of the natural changes in your physical body but because of the lack of change in your contribution to this existence. There ought to be something novel, even if it's only trying a new recipe or taking a dance class.

- Maybe you don't like to leave the house because you don't look the way you did prior to giving birth to your children or are simply gaining weight. Faded beauties think that their self-worth is nothing more than their physical appearance.

- Maybe you don't bother to buy new clothes or wear make-up, because you feel that you need to first lose weight or have cosmetic surgery before you can love and accept yourself.

Timeless Beauty

Oprah Winfrey, Meryl Streep, Angelina Jolie, Barbara Streisand, Queen Latifah and Sophia Loren are a few of the women whom I consider to be ageless beauties. An ageless beauty is like wine, each passing year she becomes more beautiful than the previous year, not because of what she looks like on the outside; no matter how physically attractive she is, but because of what she is on the inside, which exudes class, charisma, compassion and personal integrity that is authentic and alluring. There is something special about her that is irreplaceable. Who she is … is so powerful and wonderful, that she is beyond the comparisons to other women and techniques of physical improvement.

Characteristics of Timeless Beauties

- They wear clothes that express their individual personality, soul and body.

- They mesmerize and captivate people with their wisdom, ideas, empathy and compassion for others.

- They are physically and psychologically irreplaceable. You cannot put another body, face, or person in their place. Their personalities are dynamic and alluring and when they are gone they will be sorely missed.

- They are not "drama queens" or "divas" they are easy to get along with and are team players. They have a humbleness and humility about them that is breathtaking.

- They are not involved in intimate relationships where they are not honored and respected by their partners. They are either happy alone or are in a committed relationship with a man who loves them unconditionally.

- They do not try to act like, or wear attire suitable for, a woman who is half their biological age. They look healthy and enjoy being in their own skin and exude an inexplicable beauty.

- They have interests, talents and abilities that they display in a positive light. They enjoy volunteering and sharing their wisdom and life experiences with others.

- As the Timeless Beauty ages, her make-up becomes more subtle, not as a fashion statement but simply because she has learned, over time, that her true beauty need not be hidden underneath her make-up.

- She is not afraid to say "no". She has learned to honor her time on earth. She is not a people pleaser and does not allow others to impose their requests on her time.

- She is confident in expressing her own opinions, ideas, and beliefs without worrying about offending others. She is confident and wise enough to accept and respect opinions that are different from her own without feeling threatened.

- You can't figure out just why she is beautiful. She just *is*.

CHAPTER 3

▼

EMBRACE YOUR FEMININITY

History books abound with stories of women who fought for equal rights, the right to vote, opportunities for employment and promotions in male dominated fields and for comparable pay. They are still fighting for some of these now, as well as the elimination of domestic violence. Meanwhile femininity and beauty have become the reserved province of wealthy, upper class citizens and celebrities who still cherish and reflect the standard American ideal.

The average woman may view femininity and beauty concerns as a disadvantage in a male dominated society. Many women view femininity and financial success as mutually exclusive concepts. In modern society, too many women associate femininity with negative characteristics such as submissiveness, inferiority, oppression, weakness, irrationality, dependency and being treated as second-class citizens in comparison to men.

The reality could not be further from the truth. The Universe puts forth no creature vulnerable to the world without a means of creating and drawing to it what it needs to survive and flourish. A woman is most powerful when she accepts the physical reality of her existence on earth. Birds cannot survive using the same hunting techniques as fish. They must use their own unique characteristics for then their true strength and beauty radiates and allows them to subdue their adversaries. When women learn to respect their bodies, accept their authentic beauty, and embrace their feminine power and strength; they will no longer focus on what is wrong with the size of their breasts, or how many pounds they need to lose … but how they can use the body that they were born with, and the person that they are, to make a difference in the world. Femininity does not exclude intelligence, grace, integrity and strength. Being a woman does not mean that you can be treated with less respect. Being a woman does not mean that you are not as valuable or as intelligent as a man. Femininity and beauty is not about your physical beauty, but your spiritual beauty; it is not about the size of your butt, it is about the size of your heart.

Being a woman means that you are a divine spirit inhabiting a female body that is capable of releasing an egg each month, giving birth and nursing a baby into infancy. It simply means that during intercourse with the opposite sex your body receives the sperm as opposed to ejecting it. It means that genetically you are designed to have more fat cells than males and have less muscles and physical strength. However, it takes a woman's tenderness to bring a man to his knees. It takes a woman's charm to dilute the male ego and take from him what brute strength alone would only make him hold onto tighter.

There are many legal and social challenges that accompany being a woman in a male dominated society. Therefore many women have come to disassociate themselves from the art of femininity. Many women feel that because they have birth control methods this gives them the liberty to have intimate relations with a man without being concerned about the consequences of undefined sex. Some women think that because they can buy sperm from a bank, this means that a child doesn't need the influence of a father whilst growing up. They overlook the dual needs, and thus the essential provision of their own unique portion, the power of softness, the regality of grace and virtue, the unyielding strength of sweetness.

Yet some of the most prominent women in society have made a major impact on the world by expressing the subtle power and potency of femininity. They have used their instincts, intelligence and feminine finesse to accomplish exactly want they wanted. From Cleopatra to Martha Stewart, the likes of Marilyn Monroe, Princess Diana and Oprah Winfrey have succeeded in fulfilling their desires. They did not build or conquer their empires using characteristics associated with masculine behavior. Billionaire, Martha Stewart and Rachel Ray capitalized on that which many women have been fighting to disassociate themselves from—domestic issues—cooking, cleaning and sewing. Isn't it ironic that a woman was able to build a billion dollar industry utilizing her domestic skills, within those very same domains that many people devalue as "woman's work?"

The first black millionaire, Sarah Breedlove a.k.a. Madame C. J. Walker, built a lucrative business selling hair care products—not cars. I am not advocating that women should only create careers in sectors that are not male dominated; I am merely saying, "be true to yourself!" Whilst there is absolutely nothing wrong with appreciating your femininity, allow the sincere desires of your heart to lead your life whether it be piloting an airplane or raising a family. Whatever you decide to do with your life, just do it with pride and dignity. Don't concern your-self with what other people think you *ought* to do. Don't build your life around trying to please anyone but yourself. There is integrity too in choosing not to work outside of the home, to raising a family or simply seeing your mate off to work every morning. Staying home with your children, cooking dinner for the man you love and wearing sexy clothes and make-up has not gone out of style. You don't need to abandon your nurturing feminine spirit in order to prove that you can be successful in life.

The other side of the coin is that some women exploit themselves as sexual beings by crossing the boundaries from sexy to sleazy. It is a very subjective mat-ter to judge what may be risqué for someone else. Sometimes, I must admit, that I am willing to cross that line. But I won't pretend that I don't know when I am at the boundary. I know when too much of my cleavage is showing. I know when my skirt is too short, pants too tight or when I am wearing too much make-up. I know when my clothes do not flatter my figure. It is then that I usually don't feel sexy or attractive, just self-conscious and insecure.

I remember preparing to meet my significant other's father for the first time. I purchased a velvet, royal blue dress that was approximately six inches above my knees. It fitted much too tightly, accentuating the folds of skin on my back and causing my breasts to look twice their normal size. I wouldn't say that I looked sexy, classy or attractive. I looked desperate. My dress was screaming, "Please look at me." "Please like me." "Please accept me!" I asked myself, "What is your appearance saying without you having to open your mouth?" "What non-verbal message am I giving to his family about who I am?" I wasn't pleased with my answer and so quickly changed my outfit. It doesn't matter if the answer that came to my mind was true or not. The issue for me was whether or not my body and soul were coordinated and if, to my mind, they were outwardly expressing the same message.

Ask yourself whether your appearance radiates or hides who you really are. When I see a woman whose appearance shouts, "Look at me … like me … I am desperate for approval," then I know that she is not in touch with the essence of her true beauty and that she has not learned how to love herself. Once a woman begins to love herself, she respects herself and she then displays this in how she presents herself to the world.

Femininity abused, or un-used, many times is the flip side of the same coin. Some women ignore their femininity by dressing in unflattering clothes, using no makeup, and going around with unkempt hair, because they prefer to hide or ignore their femininity. There is nothing wrong with loving and accepting yourself completely and totally. Being a woman is a beautiful and wonderful experience. The legends of history tell of the many wars that have been won and lost over the love of a woman.

Get in touch with your feminine, frilly side. There is nothing more beautiful than a person who is confident and proud of whom they are whether they present themselves like Sophia Loren or Madonna. Star Jones, one of the hosts on 'The View' talk show, used to do a commercial for Payless Shoe Source. She was a voluptuous, beautiful woman. Payless was smart enough to know that she was projecting self-love that would encourage the average woman to shop at their shoe store because they could identify with Star Jones' unique, authentic beauty. Isn't it ironic that when Star Jones lost weight, she also lost her job on 'The View' and was no longer seen doing Payless Shoe commercials? I think that when she betrayed her truth and authenticity about how she had lost weight, she forfeited the faith and hope that her persona had previously given to so many women who looked up to her and, through that, felt good about themselves. Actor and author, Monique is one of the most beautiful women in the world to me because she accepts and expresses who she is, from the inside out, in a very loving, sincere, and charismatic fashion. She celebrates her unique beauty and femininity in grand style.

Jennifer Lopez's rounded buttocks became front page news and infuriated many African American women. How could the media make such a big deal about her buttocks when the average black woman is genetically designed with full rounded buttocks? Historically, black women have been ridiculed regarding their voluptuous body shape. "Why would the media promote Jennifer Lopez while ignoring black women's bodies for decades," I wondered out loud to my brother, (armchair philosopher, General George). General stated, "Many black female celebrities were very sexy when they first become popular, Toni Braxton, Janet Jackson, Angela Basset, Vivica Fox and even Halle Berry had more voluptuous figures. Due to the pressure of them trying to mold themselves to fit into the Hollywood ideal standard of beauty, they diet and exercise to tone down and get rid of what they consider to be flaws so that mainstream society will embrace them and propel their careers. The craze about Jennifer Lopez arises from the fact that she is proud of who she is. She likes herself and is not ashamed of her full, shapely buttocks.

She flaunts her body and doesn't make excuses about who or what she is. The media has come around to loving her because she loves and accepts herself and is proud of who she is culturally. Jennifer Lopez does not water herself down to fit into mainstream society."

This was a bitter pill to swallow given that I am a black woman — sometimes the truth stings. I remember wishing that I were a size three because I wanted to model. The model scout told me that my hips were too big. I was 5'7', weighed 120 pounds and wore size seven pants. I thought that I was fat and tried desperately to lose weight. I tried to squeeze my buttocks, hoping that they would disappear. Yes, black men found them attractive; but I wanted to be accepted by mainstream society. I learned that society was showing me how I truly felt about myself. To some degree, they created those feelings, but ultimately I am totally responsible for how I choose to feel about myself. I wanted society to accept and validate my body as being attractive.

I have a secret to tell you. Pull this book a little closer to your heart. Turn down the radio. Turn off the television. Take a deep breath. I want you to read this section every day until it resonates in your soul. You are the most beautiful woman in the world. There is no other woman in this world like you, near or far. You are perfect and wonderful just the way you are. You are mesmerizingly flawless. You are created as beautifully as the earth and all of its inhabitants; the trees, the flowers, the ocean, the sunset, the stars, and snowflakes. If a man, or anyone, cannot love you the way that you are; this simply means that this is not the right person for you. If you can't love yourself today, just the way that you are—you are not ready to be loved yourself.

You only need your own opinion to know that you are beautiful and successful. It doesn't matter what anyone else thinks. You're the only person who needs to believe that you are the most beautiful woman in the world. Your opinion about yourself is, for you, the most important opinion in the world. Why should anybody else think that you are wonderful, even when you don't think it about yourself? Why should somebody else's opinion about you, be more potent and important than your own opinion about yourself?

Everyone is not going to like the way that I make my chicken and noodle soup, the way I kiss, my style of writing, my body shape or size, the perfume I wear, my favorite dress, or my loud boisterous laugh; but this doesn't mean that I should change who I am. What is most important is that I love myself; that I enjoy my food and the way I kiss. My likes and dislikes are important to me. I wasn't born only to please other people. I didn't come into this world just to make other people content whilst forsaking my own happiness—and neither were you.

Whatever you believed about yourself, before reading this book, that was negative, release it. You don't need to feel bad about yourself in order to eat healthily or exercise purposefully. You don't need to verbally abuse yourself, thinking thereby that you will shame yourself into losing weight. If you tell a child that he or she is stupid, that child will begin to believe it. Remind yourself everyday how beautiful and wonderful you are and you will begin to feel that way. The world is constantly reflecting back to you, like a mirror, your truest and deepest feelings about yourself. Change your opinion about yourself, and those who matter most in your life will follow suit.

If a person told you that you were an alien from another planet, you would think that that person was completely insane. That information would not take root. You would wonder whom that person is talking about with such a ridiculously delusional perception. The reason this would not make sense to you is because you *know* that you are not an alien from outer space. You *know* this. When you know something to not be true about yourself, you are not rattled by other people's negative comments. It goes over your head like a physics lecture to a one-year-old. Like a radio station out of range it only produces an unintelligible signal. Negative information that does not already have a receptor site inside of your belief system, about who and what you are, will not resonate with your being. If you are angry or upset about another person's assessment of who you are, it is because deep down inside you actually believe this to be true about yourself, in some manner.

Many women can sit and talk for days about their own perceived flaws and imperfections. Once I went to see my good friend's mother whom I hadn't seen in 10 years. Since I grew up she had earned a bachelors degree and was working on the last year of her master's degree. I wanted to congratulate her on her recent academic achievements and talk about her journey from working at the auto plant and single-handedly raising four children, to becoming a college graduate. While hugging me, she started telling me about the protein and salad diet that she was currently on and suggesting that I try it too. Yes, we both had gained weight over the years, but she was a knockout, then and now. I couldn't bear the conversation of her weight battles, when I felt that she had overcome so many more challenging and interesting obstacles in her life.

Society's obsession with a woman's physical appearance distorts a woman's view of who she really is. Too many women think that there is virtue in constantly putting themselves down, complaining about how much they weigh, the cellulite on their thighs, their sagging breasts, stretch marks, ugly feet, the tummy-tuck that they have been thinking about, etc. Too many women don't know how to love and accept themselves, without outside validation from other people. Their comfort zone is self-criticism. I could write a thousand pages of what women dislike about themselves. If you're a woman who is not interested in talking about what is wrong with your body, you will find very few women with whom to share a meaningful conversation. So what is so interesting about constantly talking about what is wrong with the body that God gave you?

Most women want to know that you loathe yourself as much as they loathe themselves. If you don't join in on the self-berating conversation they will try to reel you in by pointing out your flabby forearms or double chin. They almost wonder out loud, "Who the hell do you think you are to love yourself just as you are!" I wonder what the world would be like if women didn't have their bodies to criticize.

I wonder what they would talk about and do with their time if they weren't constantly trying to change or rearrange their outer appearance. Instead, would there not be a tremendous amount of inner strength available for writing, singing, and painting, starting their own businesses and living the life of their dreams?

The more that I started truly loving myself, the more my soul began to disconnect from people who are self-deprecating. I don't think it's interesting or funny to hear someone constantly complain about how much weight they need to lose or gushing about who is more beautiful than they. Their thoughts are so clouded and absorbed in their negative beliefs about themselves that they can't accept or receive compliments. Positive comments do not resonate with people who don't believe that they are beautiful and successful. Their brainwaves do not receive information that does not have a receptor site operational to process that data. So if you can't believe that you are an extraordinary, wonderful, person of value, then you won't be able to hear, or accept, positive messages when someone else passes them. How can a man love you, when you find it difficult to love yourself? Women who hate other women do so because they hate themselves.

Points to Ponder

1. What does your appearance say before you open your mouth? Whom are you trying impress, attract or intimidate?

2. Do you negatively judge women who decide to remain home and raise their children instead of obtaining outside employment?

3. If you don't love and truly accept yourself then it's impossible to respect and like someone else who reminds you of all of the things that you wished that you had in your life but that you are missing. This would be most likely to apply to other women. Accepting yourself allows you to accept other people.

4. Other people reflect back to you how you truly feel about yourself. Every time you criticize another woman's clothes, body or size, you may really be criticizing yourself.

5. You are the only person who needs to believe that you are amongst the most beautiful women in the world.

6. Why should anyone else think you are beautiful and intelligent when you don't believe this about yourself?

7. Negative information that does not already have a receptor site inside of your belief system about who and what you are, will not resonate within your being.

8. Don't let society's obsession with your physical appearance distort your view of who you are inside and out.

9. Connect to women who want to talk about more than what is wrong with their body and the latest diet.

10. How can a man love you, when you have difficulty loving and accepting yourself?

CHAPTER 4

▼

NO ONE CAN BE A BETTER YOU THAN YOU

I want you to take a moment to write down everything that is wrong with your body and your life. Have a nice pity party for yourself. Acknowledge, your cellulite and fat rolls, your imperfect parents, and the boyfriend who broke your heart. Give your stretch marks and sagging breasts the proper mourning that they deserve. I want you to pour it on thick with self-pity, because if you don't feel sorry for yourself—who else will?

Personally, I am still recovering from when I discovered that Santa Claus was not a real person. My left knee only bends partially. I can't ride certain bikes or paddle boats. I have this long caterpillar-looking scar on the front and back of my left knee. For almost a year after knee surgery I was unable to bend my left knee at all. When I walked, I swung the left leg out because my knee couldn't bend. The kids in school teased me by calling me peg leg. While walking home from school in the seventh grade, I was raped behind a church down the street from my parent's home. I lost my first beauty contest when I was about 10-years-old. There were two other contestants, my 12-year-old cousin—female (thank God)—and my doll who had patches of hair missing, including all distinguishable body parts and, believe it or not, she was unable to talk. My nine and seven year old brothers were the judges and they said that I lost the beauty contest because the doll's skin tone was lighter than mine. Before my parents began working in the car factory, we were extremely poor. We had no furniture. My father slept in the living room chair and my brother, mother, aunt and myself slept in the bed that folded from the wall in the one bedroom apartment. Not to mention the boys that I loved who never called me back, even when I told one of them—my first experience of unrequited love—that I was pregnant. Did I mention the stretch marks, sagging breasts, weight gain and hair loss after having my children? Before the birth of my children, I wore a size seven. I had small, perky breasts that needed no support. Now I wear a size 14 and weight about 180 lbs. I could fill the pages of this book with stories about all the things that are not perfect about my life. We all have valid reasons to use drugs and cry about why our lives are not perfect. Have your pity party. Write down all of things that you dislike about your life.

Pity Party

Write down ten things that you specifically wish were different about your body in the space below. Then write ten of your worst experiences.

Ten things that I hate about my body are:

1. _____

2. _____

3. _____

4. _____

5. _____

6. _____

7. _____

8. _____

9. _____

10. _____

Ten of the worst things that have ever happened to me are:

1. _____

2. _____

3. _____

4. _____

5. _____

6. _____

7. _____

8. _____

9. _____

10. _____

Each time you decide that you want to feel sorry for yourself about things that have happened in the past, I want you to select a debilitating and terminal disease or disability in exchange for the body part or life event that you do not like, something that causes you to gasp with fear. What about trading places with a person who has been blind for their entire life and are not gifted musicians like Ray Charles or Stevie Wonder. Think about losing your ability to hear or see right now. Go visit an orphanage. Volunteer your time at a counseling center for rape victims. Serve food to the homeless at a soup kitchen. Spend a day with a paraplegic.

Imagine what it would be like to trade places with a person who is paralyzed from the waste down. Comfort mothers who have just lost their newborn babies. Go and visit funeral homes and morgues and watch the facial expressions of their friends and family. If you place self-pity in perspective with all the complexities of life, you will begin to understand that there is so much more to who you are and why you are here on earth. Then you will see that your life is not less than perfect, but that its perfection lies in your ability to seize the opportunities that have been presented to you so that you may positively impact the lives of others.

Next, I want you to think about all of the wonderful things that have happened to you. Think about all the wonderful, breathtaking moments that you absolutely cherish about your life and your body. Two of the moments that I cherish most are when both of my children were born. I will never forget my son's bright beautiful eyes the very first time he ever looked at me. We were still attached by the umbilical cord and he looked at me with his eyes as if to say, "So you are the woman who has been talking and singing to me. You must be my mother." I couldn't believe that something so perfect and beautiful had developed inside of my body. I was amazed at the perfection of this little human who had been kicking and moving inside of me.

My daughter was born through a caesarian section, seven weeks before her due date. The doctors told me that she would be less than three pounds and that her lungs would not be fully developed. They forewarned me that she would be placed in an incubator and need to remain in the hospital for approximately three weeks. The doctor lifted my six pounds and three ounces, sweet, little honey-stank from my uterus, screaming her little head off. Again, I couldn't believe that my body was capable of producing something so beautiful and precious. She was healthy without any medical complications.

Other moments I cherish were: The kiss the night before, my now ex-husband and I were married. I was five months pregnant; it was thundering, lightening and raining hard. We stopped the car at the corner from my mother's house to simply kiss as if we were passionate lovers meeting for the first time (second time?). I will never forget that. Completing and passing my general educational diploma on the first try after four straight years of truancy from high school. My mother gave me a huge back yard party. One of my friends said, "Your mother is proud of you, as if you graduated from high school, it's just a GED. She should be ashamed." Her comment made me feel that I had the best mother in whole world. I will never forget family vacations with my parents. My soul took in the mesmerizing scenery of the beautiful mountains outlining the highways throughout Tennessee. My brother and I threw mini-parties each morning before school that were so much fun. Oh, yeah, the night my brother and I camped out over night in downtown Detroit to purchase tickets to see Prince in concert—all three nights that he performed. I will never forget the pajama party where I felt like my soul was reunited with my best friend. I loved my first supervisor, Sue Henderson, who is now deceased; my first office with a door and the day that my boyfriend tearfully declared his love for me. I could go on forever remembering things that I love about my life. These are a few moments of time, people and events that I would never give up under any circumstances. Changing these events would be like changing the fabric design of who I am.

Now I want you to write ten of your most cherished accomplishments, events or people in your life and ten of the best features of your body.

What I love the most about my life:

1. _____

2. _____

3. _____

4. _____

5. _____

6. _____

7. _____

8. _____

9. _____

10. _____

Ten things that I love most about my body are:

1. _____

2. _____

3. _____

4. _____

5. _____

6. _____

7. _____

8. _____

9. _____

10. _____

There is one factor that many of us forget—*we* control most of the events that happen in our day-to-day lives. We control how often we talk on the phone, what movies and sitcoms we watch on television or whether or not we should watch television at all. We decide what music to buy, clothes to wear, and who should be our friends, lovers and spouses. We select which classes to enroll in, where to apply for a job and what time to go to bed and wake up in the morning.

How many natural disasters have you encountered in the last year? I am talking about major devastating events that you had absolutely no control over? The average person is not the victim of continuous life changing events. Most of us shape and mold ninety percent of our day with our own choices. Excluding illnesses, physical and mental disabilities and the call of nature most people choose a great portion of how to spend their day. In addition to shaping our day with our behavior, many of us choose our thoughts. Usually, we only remember the significant things that happen to us; we don't recall the majority of days of our lives because nothing spectacular happens. But everyday, whether you remember most of your choices or not, the choices that you consciously or unconsciously made have shaped you into being the person that you are today. Think of yourself as a work of art. A magnificent sculpture where some spots were molded and shaped with love and kindness; and other spots were sanded with abrasiveness and sharp cutting edges but that each, presently apparent, stroke is significant and was needed for you to be the unique and beautiful human being that you are today. Next, consider that for every pound that you want to lose, you must delete one of the cherished moments, objects or events listed above. What are you willing to give up to be something other than who you are?

Everyone faces obstacles regardless of their level of income or social status. Yes, Julia Roberts has been turned down for movie roles. Janet Jackson has had her own trials and tribulations despite her beauty and financial wealth. I believe there is a different type of energy that a person has when they see themselves as beautiful, just the way they are, before the world does. It's easy to think of yourself as glamorous, rich and beautiful when your records are number one, or everywhere you look you are on the cover of a fashion magazine. If your daytime talk show is number one in the Nielson ratings it is easy to believe that you are beautiful and successful. Of course it's easy to believe that you are an astonishing beauty when fans are bombarding you for autographs and screaming your name while you walk down the street. When the world is telling you how wonderful and beautiful you are, it is very easy to believe it. This is why so many people have cosmetic surgery, increase their breasts size and are constantly dieting—for external approval. However people who amaze us with their talent and beauty are people who first radiated these qualities from within, which then became outwardly manifested—not the other way around.

Comedian Monique, Rosie O'Donnell and Rosanne Barr are beautiful, talented voluptuous women. They excelled in their careers as media personalities because they believed in themselves despite what others might have thought of them. Jennifer Lopez said that early in her career one of her managers wanted her to lose weight and diet because he felt that in order for her to obtain mega success she would need to be much smaller. Lopez decided to lose the manager and maintain her voluptuous figure because she felt good about her body shape and size. Her voluptuous buttocks became her calling card to fame. She maintained her stance not because other people told her not to diet, but because she believed in herself and the already perfect shape of her body that was designed to fulfill her divine destiny.

Before the public was aware of the success and beauty of Venus and Serena Williams they were on the tennis courts practicing. When the Williams sisters initially began winning tennis games, I remember how people talked about how physically unattractive and big they were in comparison to other women. Now the media revels in the size of their body shapes, with a special love for Serena's womanly curves. These women did not change their body shape or size. They remained focused on their talents and abilities and society began to love them as much as they had always loved themselves.

You must know that you are successful and beautiful before you can convince anyone else. This has nothing to do with your physical appearance, but everything to do with your psychological attitude and belief about your own self-worth. The world can only see you as you see yourself. If you can't convince yourself that you are number one, and be your own best friend and number one fan, then you will never convince anyone else.

Harriet Tubman is my hero. When I am down I think about her life to whip myself back into shape. Harriet Tubman was born a slave. I was born free and I could legally get a free high school education. It was illegal for Harriet Tubman to even learn how to read or write her own name. She lived in a country where she was legally declared three fifths of a human being. She didn't own herself. I can imagine how she hated the degradation of slavery. She could have chosen to kneel on her knees each night and pray to God that the laws in America would change or that her master would change his mind and treat her with dignity and respect. All of this would have been wishful thinking based on the conditions in the United States at that time.

Tubman's actions indicate that she decided to wake up one morning and declare, from the essence of her being, that she was free. She had to, spiritually and psychologically; know that she was a free woman before she could physically escape slavery. Harriet Tubman's way of thinking and belief about herself propelled her into action. She did not need the laws of a racist society to tell her that she did not deserve to be a slave, or the pity of her slave master to give her the freedom that was her birthright. If you hate your body or envy the lives of other people, it is because you have not learned to cherish what is authentic and unique about your moment of time here on earth.

So if you have a thousand excuses as to why you are still at the job you detest, with the man who you know doesn't love you; and have not looked into doing the activities that you want to do or enjoy most in this world—please don't save your excuses for Harriet Tubman. She would not have wanted to hear them.

If you want to change the negative events in your life, you must also change the positive events in your life. If we delete slavery from American History, we must also delete Martin Luther King, Jr., Harriet Tubman, Abraham Lincoln and Frederick Douglas. If we delete all poverty from human history we must also delete Mother Theresa. We were born into this world to share and express a divine gift that radiates from within the essence of our being. Our physical bodies are like tools or keys that fit specific purposes. For example, Martin Luther King, Jr. needed to be a black man in America. He needed to have an appearance that was illustrative of his message of equality. He needed to look like a certain type of black man, someone to whom even white Americans could relate. He also needed to know how to articulate his thoughts into words that would transcend race and culture and open doors to heal racial concerns in America.

Queen Latifah rap artist, movie star, Oscar nominee and model for Cover Girl cosmetics, is a voluptuous beautiful woman who did not let her size prevent her from bringing her dreams to fruition. Queen Latifah is absolutely gorgeous. When people listen to the rich voices of Aretha Franklin, or Bette Midler they don't think about how small they are on the outside, but how tremendously big they are on the inside. When people focus on their special gifts and talents these qualities manage to touch the lives of so many people.

When you were created, I believe that you were given particular external characteristics such as skin color, body shape, hair length and color, height, weight, eye shape and color, lip size shape and smile. You were also designed with certain internal characteristics a particular temperament such as shyness, assertiveness, or a fondness for certain music, foods, clothes and books, a certain sense of humor, and intellectual gifts and talents—things that you are good at with little effort. For example, some people have a way with children, or making others feel good about themselves. Some will be talented at some or even all of knitting, decorating, singing, writing, teaching, dancing, drawing, painting, designing clothes, cooking or playing sports. While you are focusing your psychological energy on redesigning what is divine and wonderful about you, what you are actually doing is creating an illusion of perfection and beauty that is fake, unreal and unauthentic. This attracts people into your life who may also appear to be fake and unauthentic. The truth is, the type of bait you use to attract others determines the quality of the persons with whom you connect and the type of relationship that you will share with them.

Cosmetic surgery and dieting products are a billion dollar industry. So many women are choosing to increase the size of their breasts and lips because they think that it will make them more attractive to the opposite sex. The truth is, the man who stares at your body and ogles you, like a piece of meat, as you walk down the street, is most likely not going to be the man who is madly in love with you. The man who gives you empty compliments and stares at your cosmetically enhanced perfect body is probably not going to be the man who brings you hot tea and chicken noodle soup in the morning when you are ill. The man who truly loves you wants to feel your soft skin and warm body through and through regardless of your body's size or shape. The man who truly loves you doesn't care about the size of your breasts. A man who loves you is concerned about the depth of your integrity, honesty and love for him. A man who truly loves you loves your soul. He loves you fifty pounds lighter or fifty pounds heavier. A man who really loves you wants to love, touch, feel and caress the real you.

Do you ever wonder if fish look in the sky and say to themselves, "Why can't I fly? There must be something wrong with me." I understand the desire to look like other women, but the focus should not be on comparing yourself to other women, but thinking of ways to do more with the gifts and talents that have been bestowed upon your life.

It is not a mistake that you were born in a specific culture, a particular family in a certain geographical location, during a certain time of human existence with special gifts and talents and a certain body size and shape. All of the physical, psychological and geographical details of your life are together a part of your divine plan of perfection.

There is no one in the world that is loved or hated by every single person. Eva Braun loved Hitler; Osama Bin Laden has supporters. Some people still believe in and support O. J. Simpson. Madonna is a cultural icon, but everyone doesn't like or buy her music. Everyone doesn't watch Oprah. Everyone doesn't need to see or enjoy the same movies for it to become number one at the box office. Do you understand what I am saying to you? No woman no matter how beautiful she thinks she is, is beautiful to every person in the world. You don't need everybody to love and respect you, you just need to love and respect yourself.

Look in the mirror and apologize to your body for hating and loathing it, yet expecting it to do whatever you want it to do. Make a promise to yourself today to stop criticizing and beating yourself up for not looking like someone else. If you had a friend that treated you the way you treat yourself, you would probably eliminate them from your life. Tell yourself today, right now, as soon as you stop reading this paragraph, that you are perfect just the way you are. Admire your arms, legs, stomach, breasts—all of yourself. Love and appreciate yourself the way you would want someone else to do. No one is better than you unless *you* don't believe it.

I want you to look at your body and praise all that you see. Apologize to each body part that you have disrespected over the years. Tell it what is wonderful about it and thank it for being the vessel of your soul in this lifetime.

Points to Ponder

1. All of the good things and bad things that have ever happened to you make you who you are.

2. Changing who you are on the outside does not change who you are on the inside.

3. Think of the very best thing and the very worst thing that has ever happened to you. Ask yourself if you would be willing to give up the best thing that ever happened to you in exchange for the worst thing that has ever happened to you?

4. No one can be a better you than you.

5. Eighty percent of the decisions you made five years ago explain why you are where you are in your life today.

6. People will judge you the way you judge yourself.

7. If you lose twenty pounds, your casket will be twenty pounds lighter. If you touch twenty lives you will live forever in their hearts.

8. You can only be a cheap imitation of somebody else.

CHAPTER 5

▼

ARE YOU A SEXUAL BEING
OR A SEX OBJECT?

You've noticed that your man's attention for you has waned. His kisses feel cold and distant and when you look into his eyes—you feel invisible. You want him to compliment you by telling you that you are beautiful. You want him to notice your new hairstyle and the outfit that you selected just for him. But for some unknown reason, you can't figure out why your man is no longer interested in you. You have asked him a hundred times whether or not he is in love with someone else. Each time he tells you, "Honey, there is no one but you. Why do you ask?"

Sex with him is routine and lacks passion. If you don't initiate sex, it doesn't happen at all. Many women at this point in the relationship begin to blame themselves for not being beautiful enough, sexy enough and perfect enough to keep their man interested in them sexually. They feel that if their stomachs were flatter, waist smaller and breasts bigger and firmer, their man would still be in love with them. This is not true. People fall out of love with us for a variety of reasons that have nothing to do with our physical appearance. Usually men stop loving us around the same time that we stop loving ourselves. The best way to hold onto ourselves is by letting go of people who no longer love us—for whatever reason—with grace, peace and dignity. You cannot keep a man by gaining or losing weight. If he truly loves you then weight is not a real issue between you.

If a man cannot love you for who you are, at the size that you are now, today, at this very moment—he will never love you. You will never be good enough for him if you are not good enough for him now. You cannot force a person to love you, neither by pressure, nor by change.

If you are on a diet now because you think that this will help you find a man, keep a man or entice a man to love you more, ask yourself why you think that changing your physical appearance is going to be the key factor that determines his love and attraction for you. Why do women diet for their wedding? Is it really because they want to look good in their wedding gown? Or at a subconscious level are women using dieting as a way of feeling more worthy and deserving of the man that they are marrying?

As women, we feel that the average man is holding out for Tyra Banks and America's next Top Model. Men feel that women are holding out for the next Donald Trump and Denzel Washington. The truth is that both men and women are waiting for that special person who makes them feel rich and beautiful inside and out.

The people in your life reflect back to you how you really feel about yourself. Before you focus on losing pounds of flesh from your body eliminate unhealthy relationships from your life. What are the people in your life reflecting back to you about yourself? I hear a lot of anger when I tell people this. The truth is: The reason that you remain in relationships with people who mistreat you is simply because you love them more than you love yourself. But, the flip side of this is that, you truly don't love yourself. When you love yourself, you find it impossible to willingly and knowingly choose to remain in the company of people who do not have your best interest at heart.

Don't look for your identity and self-worth outside of yourself. Select someone because you love them and they love you in return. Whatever characteristics you seek in someone else, first develop them within yourself. Remember that like attracts like. If you want to marry a lawyer, become a lawyer. If you want to marry a doctor, become a doctor. If you want to marry a millionaire, become a millionaire. It is not a man's responsibility to pay your bills or finance your hair, nails and wardrobe. It is not a man's responsibility to buy you expensive jewelry and the house of your dreams. It is not a man's job to make you happy. You are responsible for your own happiness and well-being.

Some women diet or opt for cosmetic surgery to obtain or maintain sexual relationships because they psychologically see themselves as an inanimate object in the relationship, existing only for the pleasure of their male partners. Additionally, many women see themselves as human barter for exchange in the market for goods and services. She thinks that the more attractive she is on the outside, the more money a man will be required to spend on her. These women focus on how much the man is going to enjoy having sex with them as opposed to how much she is going to enjoy receiving and giving pleasure in a mutual sexual relationship with him. Most women psychologically view their bodies as givers and not receivers of sexual pleasure. This is why so many women have cosmetic surgery to increase the size of their breasts, lips and, more recently, buttocks. This is why women diet. Women diet because they want to be loved. They want to be the objects of men's desire.

Before a woman can be sexy to a man she must first learn to embrace her own sexuality and femininity. Your first and most important task on the journey to seeing yourself as a sexual "being" and not a sexual "object" is to find your clitoris. It is proof from the Universe that women were not merely put here as sexual tools for pleasure, but that they are entitled, and equipped, to enjoy their bodies too (more about the clitoris later.)

You can't be "insanely" in love with someone else and love yourself simultaneously. If you are a fool in love with someone else, you are clearly out of love with yourself. Don't confuse, allowing someone to exploit you emotionally, with love. If you believe that you are so in love with someone to the point where you are destroying yourself physically and psychologically … please note that what you are experiencing is not being in love with someone else; what you are experiencing is being out of love with yourself. If the relationship you are in involves physical or verbal abuse to you or your children, infidelity, the inability to maintain steady employment, alcohol or substance abuse, then immediately remove yourself from this situation. Never ask yourself why a man is treating you in a negative way; this question in non-productive and takes away your power and ability to control your own life. Always ask yourself, "Why am I allowing this man to treat me this way?" That is the question that you must ponder. Only *you* have the answer that matters. Only you have the power to make the necessary changes to improve your life.

Your body is the vehicle for your soul in this lifetime. The same breasts that your partner touches during sex are the same breasts that can sustain the life of your child. The lips that kiss your child good night, your mother 'hello', and your best friend 'good-bye' are the same lips that passionately kiss your man. There is no separation between you and your body. When you have unprotected sex with a man, you are not just hurting yourself but everyone who loves you. Your body is precious; it is the vessel that holds your precious treasures. You set your own price. What are you worth?

The degree to which you are discriminating with whom you share your body is directly related to how much you value yourself. If you owned a diamond necklace worth a million dollars and someone offered you five dollars for it, you would think that that person had lost their mind. You wouldn't even contemplate selling your million-dollar diamond necklace to this person. Too many women don't value their bodies as being divine and irreplaceable. They allow themselves to get involved with men who tell them, through their actions and words, that they do not value them. Some women complain that the man they love barely cares for them, or is cheating on them with someone else. Don't sell yourself short by spending your precious life energy with someone who doesn't reciprocate your love or feelings. Don't sell yourself short by accepting less than you deserve in a relationship. Believing that you are a valuable human being is an understatement; you are a priceless, irreplaceable divine soul.

You teach people how to treat you by what you are willing to put up with. Sometimes we think that if we love a person enough they will love us in return. It's like rewarding a child for bad behavior; each time the child runs in the street you reward him with a cookie. You are letting the child know that their negative behavior is acceptable.

> *Rewarding a man with your love who mistreats you, teaches him to continue to treat you in the same manner.*

Unless you are being held hostage or you truly fear for your life, (you have taken legal action to no avail) remember that a person is not abusing you, you are allowing yourself to be abused, for whatever reason, by choosing to remain in the relationship. Maybe you are afraid of poverty, of being single, raising your children alone or what other people may think of you. But just remember, you are making a choice to remain with someone who doesn't love or respect you. You can't pressure someone into loving you. You can't mislead someone into loving you. You can't force someone to love you. You can't coerce, trick, beg or plead with someone to love you. You can't buy love. If loving you doesn't come easily to that person, and you feel that you have to earn their love, this is not a healthy relationship.

You can't make your heart beat, command the sun to rise, or cause the rain to fall to earth. Neither can you insist that everyone enjoy your salmon pate', love your favorite song or laugh at your favorite scene in a movie. It's impossible. But what you can do is know that this world is big enough for you to find someone who adores you just the way you are. You have got to believe and know that you are worthy of someone who is capable of loving you in a way that feels good to you.

Sometimes you can be so good to a person by giving them whatever they want; whenever they want it— that the person may believe that he truly loves you. But if the giving is primarily by you, what you are mistaking for love would be better defined as need or dependency. If you feel drained in a relationship ask yourself if this person is adding or deleting joy in your life. Determine if this person is giving and sharing emotional, spiritual, social and financial resources that balance the relationship.

Your primary relationship is with yourself. You can't select the right person without being the right person; and being the right person simply means knowing who you are. Do you enjoy your own company? Can you look at your own body and admire it? If you were somebody else could you live with yourself? If you were someone else could you love and accept yourself as you are today at this moment? Do you have a healthy relationship with yourself?

Take yourself to your favorite restaurant, buy the diamond ring that you have been admiring, go on a cruise to Tahiti with a group of strangers. Use your best dishes even when no one is coming to dinner. Wear your cute black negligee to bed because you feel like it. Polish your toenails, shave under your arms and dab your expensive perfume on your favorite spots, just for you.

Why the Clitoris is Hidden

You meet a man in a bar. Tom Cruise and Denzel Washington on their best days could not compete with this stranger's charisma and physical attractiveness. His smile warms the room and you cannot believe that this man wants to get to know you better. You are a liberated woman armed with birth control pills and condoms. You don't subscribe to societal ideologies to suppress female sexuality. You 'know' that you are not a slut, tramp, whore or being promiscuous. You are in touch with your sexuality and understand that women have sexual needs and desires just like men. He wants you now. You long to feel his broad shoulders holding you. You anticipate what his kisses taste like. It is what it is, who cares if he never calls. You follow him to a little room in the back of the bar, within two minutes his body succumbs to the pleasure of an orgasm.

Being totally honest with yourself, do you think you would have had an orgasm within two minutes of sexual intercourse? Don't you think an orgasm for an orgasm is an even exchange when there are no strings attached in a sexual encounter between a man and a woman? There are exceptions to the rule, but in the majority of cases do you think the typical man provides foreplay or tries to find the clitoris when it does not directly affect his ability to receive sexual satisfaction from your body. If a man never touches, seeks, or stimulates the clitoris … he will be able to achieve an orgasm through sexual intercourse. Some women are able to achieve vaginal orgasm, but the majority are not, unless the clitoris is stimulated directed or indirectly.

Intercourse is a very sexually fulfilling act, but why do you think the clitoris is one to two inches away from the vaginal entrance? A woman does not need to achieve an orgasm to become impregnated. Have you ever wondered what the biological function of the clitoris is? Some psychologists say that its purpose is to create an emotional bond between the male and the female. Think about sex with your male partner. Who has the most orgasms during sex … you or he? Why do you think that it is biologically easier for most men to have an orgasm as opposed to most women?

If a man does not ejaculate this would interfere with the perpetuation of the human species. If men were having orgasms at the same rate as women, I believe that there would be a drastic reduction in the number of babies born around the world. Men are biologically designed to ejaculate as easily and quickly as possible because it is a necessity to propel the human gene pool into the future. Women on the other hand can have baby after baby and never experience an orgasm or enjoy sex in the least bit. Women are biologically designed to have sex whether they are physically aroused or not. In the event that a woman is raped, except in rare cases, she will not experience an orgasm. This is nature's way of detaching a woman's sexual psychological health and pleasure from sexual abuse and exploitation. The position of the clitoris allows women to detach their sexual pleasure from unhealthy sexual encounters.

The clitoris has no biologically designed function for the survival of the human species. A woman's breasts are capable of nurturing her baby. Her vagina contains the urinary tract and is the birth canal for her children. The woman's body is the receiver and giver of life.

The woman's clitoris is a gift given to her by the Creator. It is the only part of her body that does not belong to the machinery for the survival of herself or others but symbolizes her wholeness as a complete being. Some researchers have claimed that women have a G-spot inside of their vagina that gives a more intense orgasm than the clitoris. This is an attempt by a patriarchal society to lead women into believing that the male holds the magic wand that completes her deepest pleasures and desires. They bypass the obvious pleasure zone and go searching deep inside of her to find a spot that only he has the key to open. Many women feel inadequate when they are unable to achieve orgasm through intercourse. This is why more women than men fake orgasms to appease their partner's ego. A man has access to his penis and can stimulate himself manually at will. Why would nature place a woman's pleasure zone in an area of her body that is difficult for her to find? Why would nature place a woman's pleasure zone in an area that is controversial as to whether or not it even exists?

A woman's clitoris exists to let her know that she is not a baby vessel and sperm receptacle. She is a person who is capable of not only giving pleasure but receiving it as well. The clitoris' placement allows a separation between procreation and pleasure. If a man is emotionally invested in a woman's well-being, then he will want to conjure up her secret genie. He will rub the magic lantern before he enters her secret garden. He will make it a point to learn what she likes and dislikes. He will say the right words that excite her to come out and play. He will want her to know his voice and his touch. A woman's clitoris is her magic lantern that belongs to her and her alone, but the man who loves her will treasure and nurture its secret powers.

> *Having a good relationship with yourself means that you are able to treat yourself the way that you think somebody else should treat you.*

CHAPTER 6

▼

WHY WOMEN COMPETE
WITH OTHER WOMEN

Do you know why women envy and hate other women? Are you thinking that it is because she has a tantalizing body with curves that even valleys and rolling hills would envy? Is it because she is drop-dead-gorgeous and men stop breathing when she walks into a room? Is it because her smile is contagious and everyone seems to effortlessly love her? I hear women say things such as, "I can get any man I want in this dress;" "I can take her man anytime I feel like when he see my ass in these jeans;" "All the women at the club will hate me when they see how good I look in this outfit." Why do women use their looks to compete with other women?

Search your souls and be honest when answering these questions: Do women use their bodies to compete with and incite jealousy in other women? Generally speaking, do not women make comments about how their beauty or physical appearance compares to other women's, as a method of evaluating their superiority over other women? As women we have a tendency to believe that if we physically "look good" we are intellectually, morally and spiritually superior to another woman; regardless of any other attribute about our personality or achievements.

When I was about nine-teen-years-old a group of female friends and I went out to a dance club dressed youthful and provocative. A handsome young man expressed an interest in me by repeatedly asking me to dance and complimenting my appearance. The girls teased me about how attractive he was and how lucky I was to attract such a good-looking man. One girl in particular stated, "Girl, you better hold on to him with your flat-chested-ass, don't make me snatch him with these double Ds." We all laughed. I laughed too; it's just that it really wasn't funny to me. I didn't know how to respond or analyze her threat to take a guy who was interested in me because her breasts were bigger than mine. I was raised to think that this type of behavior was simply normal, acceptable chatter between women. But these types of comments never felt right to my soul. I always felt inferior or threatened by this type of banter.

Have you ever been intimidated by your boyfriend's or husband's friendship with a woman who you believe is physically more attractive than you are? You know that gnawing feeling in the pit of your stomach when you notice her flat stomach, small waistline, long shapely legs, and buttocks that you would kill for? You can't believe how beautiful she is and how, in her presence, your man pretends to concentrate on work. She walks over and introduces herself, and although she seems nice, you absolutely hate her guts. You hated her guts from the moment you laid eyes on her. There is pretty much nothing she can do to change your opinion about who she is as a person. God forbid this creature of perfection has a wonderful personality to compliment everything else nature has generously bestowed upon her. For most women it takes a half a second to size up another woman's physical assets. We feel like we know who our competition is, based on what she looks like naked in comparison to what we look like naked. We feel within our souls that, if she really wanted to, she could take our man in a heartbeat. On a daily basis most women do not compete for professional achievement, academic success, or promotions the way they compete with each other for the attention of men.

Somehow you feel that the man you love would be willing to give up every moment he ever shared with you ... just to taste her, to hold her and touch her because ... God must have awakened early in the morning to sculpt her and He pieced you together with her leftovers after six days without sleeping. She reminds you of everything that you want but could never have. Some women show envy of other women by saying that they feel that the woman is not physically attractive and does not deserve the man, job or beautiful children that she has. Some women have said that they don't understand how certain women who are "ugly" or "fat" deserve nice looking husbands who are faithful to them. They can't believe that a woman who was made from their leftovers is living the life of their dreams. Unfortunately, many women place their internal value as a human being on their external appearance. We think we can look at a person and judge whether or not he or she has integrity, honor, faith, intelligence and wisdom. We look at the outside and think we know and understand what is inside of that person. This is also how women judge *themselves*. We look at our physical body and blame it for the choices we have made in our lives. It is not our body's fault that we let a man move in with us who did not love us.

It is not our body's fault that we choose not to pursue our education or take long walks in the morning. It's not our body's fault that we choose to remain in jobs we loath. It's not our body's fault that we continue to remain friends with people we cannot trust and who have hurt us deeply in the past. It is not your body's fault that your skin crawls every time that you allow a man to have sex with you who doesn't respect you outside of the bedroom. It is our soul beckoning for our consideration. It is the part of us that we cannot see that desperately needs our attention. We look in the mirror and think we can nick, tuck, cut and diet our problems away. But no matter how many pounds we lose, we never lose ourselves. We must stop blaming our bodies for what is wrong with our lives and listen to our hearts in order to make real changes in the quality of our lives. Until we change how we think, feel, act and believe, we will never feel whole, complete and satisfied with we are.

Again, do you know why women envy and hate other women? We hate them because we think their lives are perfect. We hate them because we think that God showed favoritism when He created them; He used His best paint brushes and most superior ingredients to manifest their being. We hate other women because we think they don't know what it feels like to have a guy say, "I'll call you," while you wait by the phone for days, and he never calls. We don't think that their hearts have ever been broken by someone they loved more than themselves. We hate them because they don't appear to have experienced tragedy, loss and disappointment in their lives. We hate them because we don't think they know what it feels like to cry themselves to sleep at night because they didn't get the job or promotion that they worked so hard to earn.

We envy other women because somehow we believe that if we looked like them then our lives would be so much easier. We fantasize that if our man's fingertips fondled perfectly firm breasts and his kisses did not sink into our soft, fleshy, bellies with wiggly lines; he would love us so much more. The man we love would have a much more intense and gratifying orgasm … if only we were smaller, tighter, firmer and prettier. We think that he will enjoy her so much more than ourselves. If we were more beautiful the man we love would never tire from looking at us when we are talking to him; and never comment on how beautiful another woman is, because he would be captivated and mesmerized by our spellbinding beauty—always.

As a counseling psychologist working with women, I have discovered that one of the indirect causes of why women are disloyal to each other is based on self-hatred and low self-esteem more so than the need to hurt other women. In therapy sessions women have revealed that the reason that they slept with their friend's or relative's husband or boyfriend was not because the man was particularly appealing, but because of what the woman who had him represented. Therefore in essence sleeping with another woman's male partner was a way of indirectly possessing the qualities of the woman that the friend admired.

All names have been changed

Sonia, 33: "My relationship with my sister-in-law is putting a strain on the entire family. I hate her because my husband, her brother, is always bragging to me about how pretty and smart she is. I was so tired of hearing that sh—!" When she went on a business trip for two weeks, I asked her husband to sleep with me. His big mouth told the entire family. I denied it, but no one believed me. I got four kids and I dropped out of high school. I envy my sister in-law for getting a college education and not having a bunch of kids. Sometimes I just wonder what it feels like to be her. Her stomach is flat, she got the cutest shape. I figured that if I could get her man, then that means I am just as smart as she is."

Belinda, 28: "A female friend said to me about our mutual friend Tammy, 'We shouldn't even set our sights on the same type of man that Tammy attracts. Her body is slammin,' she can't get nothing but lawyers and doctors. With the way our fat asses look, we should be lucky if he got a job.' That hurt me so much. I can't believe that she said that to me. I love Tammy, but I couldn't help wondering if she thought she was better than me. Yep, I slept with her, boyfriend. I had to. I had to prove to myself that I am just as good as she is. I don't know why she even bothers to sleep with him, he was a terrible lover, but I am an even worst friend."

Doreen, 24: "Your friend buys a dress that you love. Right? She knows that you love that dress, but you can't wear it because your stomach is too big. Fine. Whenever, we go shopping and see the same pair of shoes that we want to buy; You guessed it, it's always in her size and not mine. She just got promoted. I am happy for her, you know what I am saying. If somebody had an ice-cream cone and was always licking it in front of your face, talking about how good it is, wouldn't you just want to try it one time? I'll will never look like Sabrina in a dress, I can accept the fact that I wasn't made that way. When we are together people are always looking at her. But when I made love to her boyfriend, I pretended that I was her because I wanted to feel as beautiful as Sabrina. I hate myself for what I did because she was my only friend. But I finally got to get something that I thought that only she could have."

When a woman buys into the social belief that her worth is attached to her physical appearance, she overlooks the true beauty that lies in the substance of her character. Becoming sexually involved with a friend's male partner is a tool of destruction that perpetuates an energy of competition and self-loathing amongst women. A woman emotionally exploits and rapes another woman by becoming sexually intimate with her male partner. Loyalty, trust, honesty, integrity, faithfulness, and honor are psychological boundaries that solidify healthy relationships with our selves and other.

When we envy other people, we don't really envy their physical appearance, we envy the love, respect and excitement that we think that looking like them would bring into our lives. When we envy another person this is simply an internal sign that something is missing in our own lives. We need to take a good look within ourselves. We should never envy another person unless we want to take on every social, emotional, spiritual, physical and psychological and financial condition that shaped them into being the person that they are. Each such person, whom we see as the object of envy, is layered with very many factors that contribute to the illusion of perfection that we perceive.

I want you to take a moment and think about two women that you have always secretly envied. Hold that thought for 10-15 minutes. Now answer the following questions about each of them.

Give a detailed description of her physical appearance:

_____

_____

_____

What were her most striking physical characteristics?

_____

_____

_____

How did other people respond to her in public settings?

_____

_____

_____

Give a description of her personality:

_____

_____

_____

What are some of her academic or professional achievements?

_____

_____

_____

Give a description of the type of relationships you have observed in her life.

_____

_____

_____

You can never compete fairly with another person. A fair competition means that each person has the same physical, emotional and psychological advantages and disadvantages and that each 'contestant' is given the same amount of financial and economic resources. Each contestant has an equal amount of social and political support. And each contestant has the same amount of strength, self-will, determination and internal motivation to win the competition. What is an upset in sports? It's when the person who we believe is physically superior or has some type of edge or advantage over their opponent fails to win the competition. We can physically observe what appear to be the visible assets with our eyes, but we feel the spiritual assets of another person with our souls. The strongest, truest and most valuable entity of another human being is never the characteristics that you can see or touch. The truest, most authentic and priceless characteristics of another person can only be perceived through our own grace, integrity and beauty as a human being. If you really want to know how beautiful a person is ... imagine who they are when no one is looking.

We create artificial rules, boundaries and guidelines to make competitions "appear" fair so that each person has an equal opportunity to win. But, no matter how many rules we create, life was never meant to be equal on the physical plan. This is why some people are born with physical and mental handicaps; some people are born into wealthy families and others are born to live destitute lives in rural and urban ghettos. Some people are born with tall, muscular thin physiques that never requires them to exercise or diet to maintain their weight; while others bodies are voluptuous and plump and no matter how much they diet and exercise they still resemble a fertility goddess. We can argue from a societal, political and economical perspective that some people are considered to be more valuable than other people because of their social status. However, if we decided to measure this person's worth by calculating their ability to love, counting the numerous lives they have touched, and analyzing their personal honor and loyalty to others; we may see their social status, physical attractiveness and human value increase on a different scale.

You can't keep a man in love with you with things that age, fade, decay, diminish, lose elasticity or die. The things that keep a man in love with you grow, flourish, blossom, expand and live forever such as love, loyalty, trust and believing in him. It is not the size, or firmness of your breasts that will keep or make a man fall in love with you, but the love and respect in the heart behind your breasts. It is the heart behind your breasts, which forgives and loves him unconditionally, that attaches him to your soul. It is your heart, mind and soul that support him when he loses his job or fails to get the promotion that he thought he deserved. What keeps a man in love with you are your integrity; self-respect and honesty which he can rely on to help him through the difficult times as well as to enhance the good times in the relationship. He loves you for believing in him when he stopped believing in himself. He loves your patience, kindness and understanding when you listen to his side of the story without judging him.

He loves you because he can count on you to tell him the truth even when it hurts, and know that you will love him just the same. He loves your compassion, sense of humor and enthusiasm for life. A man who really *loves* you, loves the parts of you that he would never want to compare with those of another woman.

Points to Ponder

1. Have you ever flirted with or tried to seduce another woman's man (you knew that they were in a committed relationship) because you felt that you were more attractive than she?

2. Have you ever felt insecure around another woman because you felt that she was more attractive than you?

3. Do you look at a woman's physical appearance, or her level of intelligence, as a gauge to determine whether or not she deserves the man whom she is with?

4. Do you blame your body size for the mistakes in your life or the reason that you are currently unhappy in your life? Do you think that you would be happy if you lost a certain amount of weight?

5. No matter how many pounds you lose, you will never lose a negative self-concept until you change the way you think, feel, and act. You will never feel whole, complete and satisfied until you learn to love yourself inside and out, including your flaws.

6. Women envy other women because they believe that if they looked like them, their lives would be easier and more fulfilling.

7. You can never compete with another person. A fair competition means that each person has the same physical, emotional, psychological and financial advantages and disadvantages.

8. The truest, most authentic and worthy characteristics about another person can only be perceived through our own grace, integrity, and beauty as human beings.

9. If you really want to know how beautiful a person is, imagine who they are when no one is looking.

10. You can't keep a man in love with you with things that fade, age, decay, diminish, lose elasticity, or die. The parts of your being that will keep a man in love with you grow, flourish, blossom, expand and live forever— love, loyalty, trust, and believing in him.

11. A man, who really loves you, loves the parts of you that he would never compare to those of another woman.

CHAPTER 7

▼

MALE COMPETITION VS. FEMALE COMPETITION

Current research suggests that women are more critical and less accepting of their physical appearance than men. Women are more critical of their appearance because the standards for female beauty are higher and more inflexible. Studies show that men are more likely to be either pleased with what they see or be neutral. Research shows that men generally have a much more positive body-image than women and tend to overestimate their physical attractiveness. Men are psychologically attached to their bodies. Men don't stop loving themselves because of a receding hairline or a beer belly.

Male Competitiveness

Men and women compete with their own sex in different ways. Men compete with each other in a more psychologically healthy manner. Men compete with other men in a fairly open, principled and fair manner. They tend to play an open game with reasonable rules of behavior and honor true, clean competition amongst themselves. They know that the clock will continue to tick as long as they are willing to play the game. They know that there aren't any rules except the ones that they create for themselves. From a societal standpoint, men compete at a more objective level where there is a clearer winner and loser and where the individual or team can alter the outcome based on their own initiative. Man against man. Will against will. The results are tangible, concrete and objective. Two men box in a ring until the finish. The contender who jabs the fastest, hardest and the longest will win. Two men design cars. Which car drives the fastest or saves the most gas wins the competition. Men fight other men in wars. The winner is determined by how many men are left alive.

Maybe the way men compete appears to be brutal, un-evolved, immature, irrational and savage-like; but it is more logical, respectable and honorable than the way most women compete with each other. Men know who their rivals are. They can see their enemies and they know who they are fighting with and why they are fighting. Men compete with each other directly.

Female Competitiveness

On the other hand, when women compete with each other at a societal level, the criteria for winning are usually set by others and the results are subjective and intangible. Women are usually judged by characteristics that they have little control over; something that they did not create, and that exist outside of themselves such as their physical appearance. Their success is based on subjective, biased, external validation by others. They can't see how to beat their rival because their rival is in no more in control of the outcome than they are. How can you really be more beautiful than another woman, when the decision is nothing more than someone else's opinion of beauty? How can you change someone's personal preference for a certain body size and shape, a particular eye color or a fondness for blondes? How many people are needed to think that you are beautiful before it is a valid or meaningful judgment? Who do you need to tell you that you are beautiful before you can believe it to be true … construction workers, truck drivers, the man walking down the street, your pastor, the Pope, your boss? Women compete with each other for male attention and compliments as if it feeds their self-worth and self-esteem. Women try to dress sexier and have shapelier bodies than other women. Women compete with each other in order to maintain a current relationship, obtain male companionship or steal another woman's boyfriend or husband. Even when women do not want to "steal" another woman's male companion they take pleasure in knowing that they made him look at her.

Women enjoy psychologically torturing each other as delicious eye candy that other men cannot resist. The more physically appealing we are, and the more men whom we can entice to look at us, the bigger the psychological advantage we have over making other women feel insecure and jealous of our beauty. We as women know this because we feel it when it happens to us. Women are so busy competing with each other for male attention that they do not have the psychological, intellectual or emotional insight to change the social climate that is causing them to suffer from low self-esteem. Women think of men as being promiscuous, unfaithful, lying, cheating dogs. But what most women need to come to grips with and understand is that research shows that a man is most likely to have a sexual affair with a woman's best friend, relative or neighbor … a woman whom she trusts, loves and respects. One of the reasons that men who cheat are so successful at it, is through the agency of women who allow them to succeed, because they are in such intense competition with each other.

Women believe that they are superior to other women if they are physically more attractive. In a commercial for a diet pill a woman bragged, "I am now smaller than the woman my husband left me for." This statement leads me to believe that she felt that she deserved her husband's infidelity when she was over weight and physically unappealing. Her motive for losing weight was to be physically smaller than the other woman that her husband left her for. She viewed the other woman as competition, more so than feeling betrayed by her husband's disloyalty. The wife's motive for losing weight was not to improve the status of her health or increase her self-esteem but to be smaller than her competition—the other woman. The weight control commercial is blatantly telling women that they need to look a certain way in order to earn their husband's love and fidelity. It doesn't matter whether or not you cook his meals, raise his kids, and support his dreams … what matters most in a relationship is whether or not you are physically attractive enough to keep your man at home. There is an assumption that it is natural for a man to cheat on a woman who he feels is no longer sexually appealing. Many women believe that it is their fault when their husband or boyfriend cheats on them.

Many women say, "She looks too good for him." What they are really saying is that with her level of physical of attractiveness, she should be with a man who has more power, wealth or status in society. Women tend to subconsciously believe that if a woman is extremely attractive, the assumption is that the man will have a more enjoyable experience making love to her because of her beauty; therefore her vagina is more valuable and can be purchased at a higher price. I once counseled a woman who said, "When I lose weight I plan to leave my husband because I'll be more attractive to other men who have more money." Do women really want to steal or attract male attention because they truly love, desire or want the men? Or do women seduce, entice and flirt with men as a method of competing with other women? Women compete with each other indirectly through spreading gossip and rumors, emotional manipulation, and other backstabbing, under-handed methods.

A man can build a faster airplane, a more efficient car, work on his jab for his next fight in the boxing ring or create a new marketing strategy for his business. A woman can do all of these things just as well or better than a man; but the reality is that from a societal perspective, she will be valued more for her physical attractiveness than any of her other assets, talents or contributions to society. The most disturbing aspect of this situation is that a woman has the least amount of control over what other people think about her level of physical attractiveness. A woman's perception of self-worth is validated outside of her self from others and this affects her internal psychological concept of her own value as a human being. Women compete indirectly with other women because they have not learned how to recognize and channel their internal desires, feelings and goals into physical, tangible realities. On the other hand, a man's self-worth is created inside of himself and this belief is physically manifested in the outside world via the achievement of his goals, dreams and desires. Once women learn that they cannot control or live vicariously through their children or the man in their life; they will stop hating each other and focus on their individual unique gifts and assets.

The following dialogue was edited from a variety of websites discussing how women relate to each other. This website discussed why women hate other women.

> "Women simply don't care if the guys are taken. They are self-absorbed and only want things for themselves no matter the cost. Although I used to believe this was more of a guy's attribute—but now I realize guys tend to have more respect towards another guy if the girl he likes is in a relationship. He would "step aside" and not break that invisible but known male bond. It's like a secret honor code that they uphold. Unlike girls. WE HAVE NONE. **We have no honor code.** We have no bond. It's every woman for herself. Sad, but true."

> "We compete against each other—sometimes not so subtly. We try to dress better, look better, snatch better-looking guys, get a better job, etc. Even though the cheating rate is higher among the male species, but you have to think about this: why would the girl let the guy cheat on his own girlfriend with her? Well, of course, let's just say the girl doesn't know he has a gf, but even if she did, that would make her "the other woman" and most likely, she'd be fine with it. It's like "AH hah! I got your man, what are you gonna do about it!?" It's the **satisfaction** of knowing that she has another girl's property—that's enough to keep her coming back to the guy. Certainly, I blame

the guy for cheating in the first place. But sometimes I feel that it's not entirely the guy's fault. It's 80/20."

"Girls will do anything to get a guy's attention—with disregard to the fact that he's married or taken; things like dressing slutty in front of someone's husband/boyfriend. They are well aware of the guy's status but do they care? Never. KIISFM had this whole cat fight this morning about that girl Crystal dressing like a slut at a gathering or something like that. I missed the whole story, but a listener called in and asked Ellen if she'd feel uncomfortable with her husband in the presence of such a girl like that. She said she would be. Of course, we would be uncomfortable. Why would we not? We know that the whore is doing whatever she's doing on purpose. At least have some respect to your co-workers, friends, or acquaintances."

"Personally, I would not dress like a slut to go anywhere, let alone an event with other couples there. Some girls are just born attention whores. But just because I know that such girl is doing it on purpose — dressed like a slut so guys will go gaga over her—I will automatically lose total respect for that girl. Guys will always look—no matter if you're butt ugly. If you got boobs, you will be stared at. Guys are just that shallow. But in terms of dressing like a slut in front of other women's boyfriends/husbands *on purpose? It's just wrong.* ANY woman with the presence of her man would be bothered. I mean, it's just like having table manners in the company for others. Same concept. It's all about having consideration for others."

"I don't like it when my boyfriend looks at other girls and comments on how hot they are. Real life or TV or magazines—makes no difference. I admit it. It's a natural response among girls. Girls like being "the other woman" — thus, if we let our man go gaga over *that other girl,* that means we let *that other girl* "win" this so-called underlying competition. That's the most sense I can make out of it all."

"Personally, I've had bad experiences with girls myself back in the early days— elementary to high school—to the point where I just said to myself: that's it. We were kids … who cares. But in junior high, my supposedly good girl- friends went after the guy(s) I had my eyes on. One of them even had the balls to write the guy love letters in their language so I wouldn't understand them in case they ever fell into my hands. This continued in high school. I had two best friends who knew I had a thing for this guy in class but they both went behind my back and flirted with and dated him. Yeah, go figure. Now, I learned my lesson, so in college I decided I only want guy friends to prevent this kind of evil, conniving female behavior."

"Girls handle things so much differently than guys … in school if you get into an argument with a girl then all of the friends of both individuals have to choose a side. Girls talk about each other behind each other's back to try and ruin reputations. Send mean cold looks across the room that make you want to shrivel up into a little ball. Guys just fight or wrestle and it's usually over for them. And that is if the guys don't forget that they are mad at each other first. They move on, but girls have to strategically attack the other in a way that will affect them for much longer than just getting in a fight and having a few bruises. We seem to hold on to the anger and resentment much longer than the males."

Intellectually, most people understand that it is treacherous to sleep with a friend's male partner. But emotionally, some of us do not see our own role in contributing to this type of betrayal. Listed below are eight suggestions on how to set boundaries between your best friend and your man.

Girlfriend Etiquette

1. Mothers have told us over the years that if a woman is consistently in your home she is after your man or your business. There is a place and time for girl-talk. No woman should be at your home visiting during the work week while you are preparing meals or spending quality time with your husband or boyfriend. Unless she is invited to dinner with a male partner or you are fixing her up with a male friend your home is sacred and should be respected as such. Pay attention to your own behavior with your female friends.

2. When you are un-escorted by a male partner it is wise to be conscientious of the message you are sending to your friend's male partner. Is your skirt extremely short, cleavage showing, belly out, nipples showing? Come now ladies, do you present yourself in a manner that shows respect to your girl-friend? Or do you blame her male partner for not controlling himself or act-ing like a "dog?" Do you bring up inappropriate conversation about sex and your male partners? What vibes are you sending out? We are not talking about male responsibility here; we are talking about being aware of human nature. It is okay to dress provocative when you and your girlfriend are both with male partners because the male energy between the two men will have balancing effect.

3. Don't invite yourself along as a third wheel on your friend's vacations, mov-ies, dinners or concerts with her male partner. Remember, she loves you very much; chances are she will say yes. Be considerate of her relationship and give her the same respect and space that you would want and need. No mat-

ter how long the couple has been together, chances are her man is not looking forward to sharing his lady's attention with you.

4.   Unless your man is calling your friend's home looking for you (under extreme circumstances), your man and your female friends have no reason to have long in-depth conversations while you are not present. Their conversations should be polite and cordial. Your friend should not be in the middle of arguments and spats between you and your male partner. She is supposed to be your ace-boon-coon, your comrade— not his. Loyalty is very difficult if there is not an underlying single agenda. Your friend knows about the cute guy who you almost gave your phone number to. The only thing she has in common with your man is YOU. One thing leads to another, don't set yourself up for a three-way-relationship.

5.   Don't think that your man would not be attracted to your female friends because you are more attractive than they are. What makes a person attractive is very subjective. Mother has always said: It is not the woman that he openly says that he likes and compliments her appearance that you should worry about, but the woman who he constantly calls unattractive and puts down is the one you should be concerned about. This may be his way of throwing you off of his scent and denying his own attraction to her. Yes, you can trust your man. He is around beautiful women all day. Just remember that he is a human being first and a man second. You don't have to touch fire to know that it can burn. Trust that he will honor and respect your relationship, but don't be naive.

6.   Should you tell her if you know that her male partner is coming on to you and you have done nothing to solicit this type of behavior? Follow your heart. Limit contact with her when she is spending time with her man. In many cases, intuitively a woman senses when her man is attracted to another woman; don't become the scapegoat for her relationship.

7.   Watch what you tell your man about your girlfriends ladies. He doesn't need to know the size of their vaginas, what the guys at work say about her and any of the personal details about her private life. Think about some of things that you have shared with your man about your girlfriend, thinking that he will see her as a "tramp." This will back fire. Giving him this information can make her more interesting and appealing. Secondly, stop sharing with your girlfriend's information about your man's sexual technique. You have

to be responsible for setting boundaries, this is about trust. When you tell your friends everything about the intimacy between you and your man you exploit the sacredness of the bond in your relationship. Many times our friends do not cross our boundaries, we let them in.

8. If you know in your heart that you are attracted to your friend's male partner. Be honest with yourself and don't seek opportunities and excuses to be around him, unless you are willing to sacrifice the friendship. If you know that he is attracted to you, distance yourself from him. It is not the mere sex that makes becoming involved with a friend's mate so heinous, it is the loyalty, love and trust that your friend has bestowed upon you that is shattered. When a woman shares her deepest, darkest, most intimate secrets with you, she trusts that you will not use it against her to usurp her man.

Points to Ponder:

- You can never stop a man from looking at or admiring another woman's beauty. You can change the way you feel about a man who disrespects you. You can choose to not feel jealous or envious. Do you really feel that another woman is more valuable as a human being than you are, simply because of her physical appearance?

- You are more than your physical body. What else do you have to contribute to humanity?

- You cannot control what other people think of you. Once you fully accept the truth that you have no control over other people's thoughts about who you are or how you should live your life; you will be free to design your own life from the inside out.

- You should never compete with anyone but yourself.

- The only person who you can control is yourself ... period.

- Whatever you seek in other people, develop in yourself. You don't need to marry a doctor—become a doctor.

- You are the most important person in the world who must believe, acknowledge and recognize your own authentic and unique beauty. Why should anyone love and respect you more than you love and respect yourself.

Why it's Difficult to Love Your Self

We live in a world that teaches us that we can only be validated by the opinions of others. If you think you are beautiful, people will say that you are stuck-up and conceited. If you believe that you are intelligent, people will say that you are a "know-it-all." If you have confidence in yourself people will say that you are cocky or have a big-head. True success and beauty is first validated within the individual.

*Resist a*sking:

- "Do I look fat in this?"

- "Is my butt too big?"

- "Do you think she is pretty?"

- Resist looking in the mirror to criticize your face or body.

- Resist criticizing other women's physical flaws. What you do to others, you do to yourself.

- Resist allowing others to make fun of you by calling you derogatory names.

- Resist calling yourself stupid.

- Resist calling yourself fat.

- Resist putting yourself down each time you make a mistake.

CHAPTER 8

▼

WOMEN RULE THE HEART & HOME

Food is a part of the way we express our family traditions, customs and culture. Food is the catalyst for our joy making, the kernel of how we celebrate our holidays and all festivities. Each ingredient has a history of its peoples' beliefs, their struggles, their dreams and their geographical past and journey. When we talk about food, we are not merely talking about nutritional substance for the physical body, but deep traditions that are in place to nurture the human soul and how it relates to others.

We have been classically conditioned to associate certain smells with particular time periods and people in our lives who matter most to us. When we smell our mother's or grandmother's meat loaf, tea biscuits or apple pie, for many of us this arouses a feeling of love and connectedness to our culture and family. We remember special events, family picnics, romantic dinners, farewell luncheons, slumber parties, weddings, funerals, Christmas, Thanksgiving, Hanukah or whatever special holidays that we celebrate. All cultures share some type of festivities that are expressed and shared by the preparing and eating of special foods. The type of food that we eat expresses who we are from a mystical, creative and rich perspective of cultural history. Imagine how boring the world would be if we did not have Chinese, Mexican, Irish, French, Italian, Greek Indian or Soul/African American food to tantalize our taste buds.

From a psychological perspective, one of the main reasons that American people are physically larger than in the past is because we no longer value or appreciate the significance of food and its relationship to family tradition, culture and humanity. Food is no longer tied to family togetherness, but is mass-produced by restaurants and fast food establishments. In the past, relatives and friends sitting down to eat together were an essential expression of family values and togetherness. Families that eat and prepare dinner together have more opportunities to touch and maintain eye contact, which increases trust and familiarity. During dinner parents have the opportunity to hear the mundane and funny things that happened to their children while in school. Children can help their parents set the table and learn to prepare traditional foods. Setting the dinner table, preparing the food and washing the dishes after the meal are all activities that create opportunities for the family to bond and share values and traditions. Food has lost its roots in the soul of human relations.

Many children live in single-parent or two-parent-working homes where most of the food consumption is purchased from fast-food restaurants. Many working adults eat muffins and doughnuts while chatting with coworkers. So many people pick up and hurriedly eat fast food on the way home from work or school. The food has no meaning; its essence becomes a part of a hectic routine to fulfill biological, but not psychological hunger. Therefore, people are consuming more unhealthy calories from eating fast foods that contribute to their bodies being physically bigger on the outside; yet more empty and unsatisfied emotionally because the food lacks cultural or familial meaning. For example, most fast food recipes are not passed down from generation to generation or filled with ingredients rich in family tradition and heritage. The recipes are tested with marketing control groups who focus on pleasing the masses for maximum profit. Many people attempt to fulfill the emptiness in their hearts through cosmetic surgery and diet products. They think that by reshaping the outside of who they are; they will change who they are on the inside.

There are many cook books and diet plans that provide recipes to eliminate or decrease carbohydrates from consumption claiming that it is unhealthy. In satisfying the trinity of the mind, body and soul— meat and poultry nourishes the body, vegetables and fruits stimulate the mind and carbohydrates soothes the human soul. The reason that carbohydrates sooth the human soul is because it is one of the main food sources where its distinctive preparation reflects the culture and family tradition of the people who cook it. Bread, pasta and desserts do not grow directly from the ground and are not born; they are created from the human soul. I know this is not an all-inclusive list, just a small example to show the significance of the relationship that humans have with food.

We socialize children to clean their plates even when they tell us they are full. This teaches children to disconnect their mind from their body to the point that they are no longer able to recognize their natural body cues for hunger. We reward children for good behavior with candy and cookies. Many teachers reward students who do well in school with pizza parties. We celebrate birthdays by giving others a beautifully decorated cake. In most societies, food is given as a positive reward for good behavior. We give Santa Claus cookies and milk for a hard night of delivering gifts all over the world. We express love, appreciation, and celebrate life with food. If food were put on earth to merely nourish our bodies there would be no point in spices, or decorations, or saucy recipes. Humans would eat their food the way animals in the wild have been eating theirs—raw blood, hair, fur, guts and all. Yuk! Even when animals in the wild eat, many of them "share" the meal. Food satisfies a biological and psychological need for many living organisms.

Women Rule the Kitchen

Your toughest competitor and critic will be none other than the woman who prepared your man's food during his developmental years. It doesn't matter if she was a good or bad mother, it doesn't matter if she is living or dead; it doesn't matter if she was an absent mother or apart of his life on a daily basis—his mother is the template and prototype of what a woman should or should not be like, burned into his brain. Her mere presence or lack thereof, through osmosis has conditioned him into his beliefs about women and their role in his life. His mother is the first woman to satisfy his emotional and physical needs. She is the first woman that he stared at adoringly. His mother who may or may not be beautiful to you—is the woman who has set the standard of beauty by which he will measure other women in his life. Will you cook his favorite dish as good as his mother? Will you do laundry and fold his clothes like his mother? Will you be able to understand and maneuver the little idiosyncrasies of his personality like his mother? His mother, grandmother, aunts, sister and other females relatives have defined womanhood for him through interaction such as eating, sleeping, playing, performing chores, watching television, down to simply deciding who should sit in the front seat of the car. They will tell him to look beyond your beauty and drop-dead gorgeous body to see the real you. They will refer to you as a slut or good-girl. They will tell him all of the dirty little secrets that women share about the virtues and hidden agendas of other women. Contrary to popular belief, women are more likely to refer to each other as bitches, tramps, whores, and sluts more so than men do in everyday language. Women are more likely to look at another woman's clothing and call her a slut or tramp because she is jealous of this woman's physical attractiveness. She fears that her male partner may become aroused by the physical appearance of a beautiful woman, so she verbally attacks her in order to tarnish his image of her.

In most traditional families it is the women in the family who prepare the food for family festivities. The women gather in the kitchen to discuss, debate, evaluate and determine not only who is going to make the biscuits and wash the dinner dishes, but also which women are worthy to become a part of the family clan. While chopping onions, peeling potatoes, and kneading dough, these women will discuss the clothing of all of the women who attended the last family gathering, the length of time that some women flirted and chatted with the male family members; and which marriages and relationships should be salvaged or terminated. These women will decide while washing and drying the dishes, sweeping the floor and putting the leftover food in the refrigerator whether or not your marriage with your man should be saved through their intervention of wisdom, love, and support; or whether or not they should give him ten reasons why he should not propose marriage or break off the engagement. The women in his family can heal or destroy this relationship with you. Housekeeping, cooking, and mending are the chores that bind the apron and heartstrings of a man to his feminine ideology. The women who performed these tasks in your man's life will remain constant; they were his first and will be his last loves. You must figure out where you fit into this web of women is his life.

And though we women never talk about the influence that our female family members have on impacting the quality of the relationship that we have with the man in our lives, we acknowledge the power that women, in general, have over the men in *their* lives.

Not only can we take another woman's husband, we can also take away her male child. You are the woman who is going to take her little boy away from her and possibly break his heart. You are the woman who could possible turn her little boy against her and break her heart. You are the woman who could possibly make better fried chicken, cream-of-wheat and French toast than his mother. You are the woman who can deny her access to her grandchildren.

Answer and discuss the following questions with other women to assess the hidden power that female relatives have in determining the quality of the relationship that you have with your male partner. In addition, based on your answers to the following questions evaluate if the women in your male partner's life is likely to support or destroy your relation with him during difficult times.

His Female Relatives

If applicable, did his mother (primary female caregiver this may include grandmother, aunts, sister or nanny) try to establish a relationship with you? In what way did she reach out to you or in what ways could she have reached out to you but chose not to?

1. Is she friendly to you over the phone? (This is a very telling sign of how his mother feels about you.)

_____

_____

_____

_____

_____

_____

2. Does she talk to you about issues that do not concern her son? Give examples.

_____

_____

_____

_____

_____

_____

3. Is she critical of your ideas, clothes or goals? Give examples.

_____

_____

_____

_____

_____

_____

4. Do you intuitively feel that his mother likes you and supports your relationship with her son? (Trust your gut feelings).

_____

_____

_____

_____

_____

_____

5. How would you describe his relationships with his mother? How often does he talk to her? Does he speak fondly of her? Ask him three of his favorite memories of his mother?

_____

_____

_____

_____

_____

_____

6. Write a brief biographical summary about his mother. Include the type of jobs that she has held and her highest level of education.

_____

_____

_____

_____

_____

_____

7. How do you think that his mother feels about her relationship with his father?

_____

_____

_____

_____

_____

8. How does your male partner feel about the quality of his parent's relationship? Does he want to emulate their relationship? If not, why?

_____

_____

_____

_____

_____

_____

9. If he has sister(s) or female cousin (s), write a brief description of each close female, her dress style and the type of men that she dates. Note whether or not he has a close relationship with his sister and how you think that she may feel about your relationship with him.

_____

_____

_____

_____

_____

_____

CHAPTER 9

▼

How to Love Yourself
as You Are

You were born into this world with the perfect body with which to obtain the desires of your heart. You are the ideal physical personification to marry the man of your dreams, create the career that you want and attract everything that you need. You have been given what you need, maybe not what you think you want, but surely what you need to fulfill your purpose in this life time.

Oprah Winfrey is a prime example of this truth. Oprah does not fit into the stereotype of the ideal mode of beauty that is promoted and revered in modern American society. She is not petite. She does not have blond hair, blue eyes or European facial features. Oprah Winfrey's success is phenomenal, to say the least. She battles with her weight, just like the average woman. Oprah may or may not realize this, but her appearance is the outer packaging of her unique gift that enables her to reach into the homes and touch the hearts of millions of insecure women five days a week. Women allow Oprah into their hearts and homes with their families while they eat dinner and high caloric desserts at the dinner table.

There aren't many female celebrities that women would allow into their sacred space five hours a week without feeling psychologically threatened by their beauty. However, Oprah's beauty is not an illusion of perfection, but an example of divine gifts that changes and transforms as she grows spiritually. What Oprah perceived as a weight problem is actually a divine gift. She has currently lost weight because it may no longer be needed to fulfill her purpose of inspiring, motivating and touching the hearts of millions of women all over the world. She may think that she is in control of her weight but there is a divine energy that will shape her to meet the needs of the hearts that she is on earth to inspire in some manner. She has aged with grace and astounding beauty that inspires the self-esteem of so many women in a non-threatening, elegant manner.

The average woman could not tolerate Halle Berry, Christie Brinkley or some supermodel type, on a daily basis, discussing their beauty and exercise regime. Supermodel Tyra Banks exposed her body flaws to her female fans and viewer, as a way of connecting with their souls and the plight of the average woman who lives outside of an airbrushed image of reality. Subconsciously the average woman can only tolerate supermodels in slithers, while leafing through a magazine or as a one-time viewing being a guest on a talk-show, or maybe seen occasionally, whilst driving on the freeway, plastered up on a billboard. To be invited into a woman's home five days a week she must humble herself by exposing her imperfections.

God gave Oprah the perfect body to do what she came to earth to do. Even her obsession with her weight is a part of her unique gift. Oprah's beauty cannot be duplicated because it radiates from the essence of her being. Iyanla Vazant, Venus and Serena Williams, Queen Latifah, Aretha Franklin, Patti Labelle, Ellen Degeneres, Jennifer Hudson and Rosanne Barr do not exude standardized beauty, as accepted by American society, but it didn't stop them from succeeding. You can't dye your hair, increase the size of your breasts or lose weight to compete with *them*. Perfection is what you already are. You dilute the potency of your beauty by imitating others and trying to be what you are not. Spend your life energy on being good and seeing the good in others; this guarantees that you will maintain your own perfection.

I wish that I had a simple reason to give you as to why I decided to accept my body as it now is; such as I lost weight, I had breast surgery, I am lifting weights daily or that some guy gave me a compliment in the grocery story. Unfortunately I don't have such simple attestations that would allow you to see an easy pathway to where you too could look into the mirror and love yourself just as you are. The simple truth is that I became tired of not liking myself. What good would it do me to criticize the body that bore my beautiful children; the body that pulled all-nighters studying for exams; the body that worked three jobs during under-grad; nursed my baby and is the receiver and giver of intimate passion and love in my relationship with my significant other. This body doesn't deserve my disdain and psychological abuse. It deserves my respect and love.

This is the body that I was born in; and this is the body that my soul will exit when it is time to leave earth. Why should I criticize it and put it down? Why would my body, my physical self, the vessel of my soul, deserve to be mistreated and criticized on a daily basis? I am tired of comparing myself to other women. I am tired of wishing that I was anything or any one other than who I am. I have learned to love me. I am not going anywhere. These eyes that greet me each morning have been here all of my life. I am sorry that it took me so long to appreciate my own beauty, my own truth and my own power. Through trial and error, I have learned to love myself. I finally realize that in this lifetime, my soul has nowhere else to go.

I realize that my body is ripe like a juicy plum. I am no longer green and firm like the freshness of spring. I am sultry and beautiful like a colorful, rich summer day. This is wonderful. This is who I am. I don't need a flat stomach, or different breasts or firmer thighs to be beautiful. Just as mist turns into rain, so rain changes to snow; each stage is as wonderful as the next. Each day I am more beautiful, more intelligent and wiser than the day before. How could I not be beautiful when I see so much beauty in the world? Surely, God didn't forget about me.

My soul-mate, will tell you who the most drop-dead gorgeous woman in the world is; my children will tell you who the most beautiful mother in the world is, my mother will tell you who she thinks should have won every beauty contest I ever entered. My brothers will tell you who has the best looking sister in the world. All the people who truly love me know how beautiful and magnificent I am. The reason that they know how beautiful I am is because they love me inside out. They love my loud raucous laugh and dark sense of humor. If you don't love me, why should I care what you think of me? It's amusing that men find me attractive, but it's meaningless. My true beauty radiates from my soul. My true beauty is reflected in the eyes of my children, when they swear that no one—but no one—can microwave frozen dinners or make peanut butter and jelly sandwiches better than I. I feel breathtakingly beautiful, when my soul mate who has seen my nude body and made love to me a thousand times is anxious to make love to me as if it were for the very first time. I am beautiful because my life is filled with joy and happiness by people who will still love me when my physical being ceases to exist.

The beauty of my soul will remain with them throughout this lifetime because I loved them. My words and deeds will fill their hearts when my body no longer exists. My beauty is untouchable, at least to the people who really matter. So remember, your true beauty never fades. It is not found in beauty contests or a new pair of breasts. It is not validated by men making catcalls while you are walking down the street. It is a belief that you are a unique, divine human being, created in the likeness of love and perfection; it is the way you feel about yourself and how you display love and respect to others.

What is Beauty? Your true beauty is an attitude. You are as beautiful as are your thoughts. You are as beautiful as your actions. Beauty is a deed well done. Beauty is the way you decorate your home. Beauty is what is on the inside expressed on the outside. Beauty is when you speak to strangers, just because they're humans. Beauty is when you smile for no reason. Beauty is when you recognize, compliment and validate the beauty in others.

Start loving yourself now by practicing the following tips:

- Forgive yourself for mistakes you have made in the past. Let go of things that you cannot change.

- Stop calling yourself by derogatory names such as stupid, fat, ugly and crazy. Stop verbally abusing yourself, this type of behavior does not inspire or motivate you to change. Putting yourself down only breeds self-hatred.

- Tell yourself daily, while looking in the mirror, "I love you."

- Accept everything about yourself right now, your personality quirks, body shape and size, strengths and weaknesses. Remind yourself that the Creator does not need an eraser.

- Say "no" when something is not in your best interest. Honor your soul by doing what is right for you. Don't become obsessed about hurting someone else's feelings whilst ignoring your own. This is not healthy—neither for them nor for you. Over time you will grow to resent the people you love, if you do not set boundaries in the relationship.

- Don't exercise to lose weight. Move your body and enjoy life. Lead an active life style because it is fun. Take walks and soak in the scene with your heart. Focus on enjoying your body and life. Your natural size for your body will take care of itself.

- Eat a well-balanced healthy diet, not because you are trying to get rid of unwanted pounds. Eat a healthy diet because of the nutritious benefits that you want to gain. Focus on the taste of fresh fruits and vegetable.

Find foods that you actually enjoy eating and that are good for your body as well.

• Refrain from interacting with people who bring you down emotionally, such as drama queens and people who are constantly depressed. Listen compassionately and encourage them to seek help, but don't let their problems become your own. If they continue to repeat the same mistakes and patterns over and over again, they are spiritually stagnant. There is nothing you can do. Love yourself enough to eliminate your time with people who are not ready to try to be their highest and best self. You may be pulled down to their level rather than being able to gather the energy to lift them up to yours.

• Lotion or oil your body daily after a shower. You should know your own body intimately. Nurture and take care of your physical self as you would take care of a baby.

• Find a way to spend time alone. If you are constantly around other people whether it is your family or friends with whom you share wonderful relationships, you may lack the time that you want to be alone, in order to recognize your own needs, thoughts and desires. Quiet your mind to get in touch with who you are.

• Don't compare yourself with anyone else. That is the quickest way to erode your self-esteem. You will never be them and no one could ever be you. Whenever you find yourself comparing yourself with anyone, immediately stop and chant three wonderful things about yourself. You are not an imitation you are the one and only original.

▼

CHAPTER 10

HOW TO DEVELOP A HEALTHY BODY IMAGE

The only truth about your life from the moment that you were born is that you were meant to die. The liposuction, silicone breasts, and smaller stomach from surgery will all remain on your corpse that leaves this earth. There are so many women who opt to have breasts surgery to entice and attract the attention of men who do not love them. She revels in his comments about how beautiful and attractive she is. She feels desired, wanted, sexy and cherished by men … But these men are not the men who will bring her hot tea or a bowl of soup when she is sick.

When a woman exposes her nude body for a million men to sexualize and adore her, she usually exploits and destroys the love of the one man who really loved her. Sometimes as women we value the opinions, the 'oohs' and the 'awhs' and the adoration of the men who didn't see us before we put on our makeup in the morning. We overlook the sincerity of the man who embraces our warm body that comforts him while he sleeps. We think that the number of men who find us attractive makes us more lovable and valuable as human beings. But it is not the quantity of men who find you attractive when you look your very best that matters, but the quality of a man who adores you when you look your very worst.

When I watched the movie Monster's Ball, I wondered how Halle Barry and Billy Bob Thornton's spouses felt. I wondered if they felt that the intimacy in their lovemaking had been externalized and diluted by sharing what was suppose to be sacred with the public.

Angelina Jolie, Marilyn Monroe, Elizabeth Taylor, Jennifer Lopez and Halle Barry have been revered as some of the most beautiful women in the world. Both men and women adore them. So why weren't they able to maintain long-term, stable, healthy relationships? Human beings are complex. These questions can only be answered by knowing who they are on the inside and analyzing the psychological and social conditions that shaped them to be who they are and why they were attracted to certain men. Physical beauty is not enough to maintain a healthy relationship. Physical beauty is not enough to make a man remain sexually faithful to you.

If a woman chooses to have children her baby won't mind the size of her breasts. So many women look for external validation of their self-worth that they do not take into consideration the importance of accepting their unique body shape and size. The most important characteristics about who you are will never leave this earth. Harriet Tubman will always live in my heart. The things that people will remember about you the most is not what you looked like on the outside but the lives that you touch, the good that you have done, your laughter and the joy that you have shared with others.

Beauty & Self Image

The economy is fueled by our insecurity. Our need to be somebody other than who we are has fueled a billion dollar industry of products designed to make us more desirable human beings. They attempt to sell us the car that will make us more desirable to strangers on the street, the expensive perfume that is guaranteed to attract love to our lives, and the diet pill that works while we sleep? If we felt good about ourselves commercials and advertisement wouldn't work. Perceived human flaws are a part of our divine protection.

My husband at the time, thought that my body was sexier after the birth of our children; however I couldn't hear him because I chose to listen to other women and to the media telling me that I needed to wear a smaller size. After having my children, my breasts size increased and their firmness decreased. Not, exactly what I was looking for when I prayed for bigger breasts. I hated them. They were hot and sweaty in the summer. I developed deep dark dents in both shoulders from wearing boulders to hold up my breasts and make them look firm. While nursing my daughter, she would hold on to a roll of skin around my waist and gently move it up and down to the rhythm of her suckling. The roll of fat that I thought was disgusting provided comfort to my sweet little baby girl. She snuggled her tiny self into the folds of my body perfectly. I wanted my body to look great for people who would never know how beautiful and special I really am. I wanted to impress strangers passing bye on the street who would look and think, "Wow, she has a great shape!" I wanted to impress people who didn't matter; and people who don't know me or love me. But my little pumpkin, loved the fullness of my body and the way it nurtured her. This was special. This was beauty. This was true love.

Sometimes I wished that my breasts didn't lay so flat to my chest. I remember when they were pointy and I could wear spaghetti straps and go bra-less in my skimpy summer clothes. But, even then, I wished that my breasts were bigger. I can't think of a time when I didn't believe that something was wrong with me that a good diet, exercise or the right girdle couldn't fix. When do we ever learn to love and accept ourselves? How many people do we need to hear say that we are beautiful for us to believe it? How many opinions does it take to validate our own self-worth for us to believe that we are valuable human beings? How many times do we have to hear that we are beautiful, successful, wonderful creatures for us to own it? Who has to say it, for us to know that it is true? We do! We must validate our own beauty, our own self-esteem and our own dreams. No one owes us. We owe ourselves.

For the most part, the majority of people are as screwed up as we are. They are searching outside of themselves for what is inside of their souls. The person who is 5'7' and 104 pounds wishes that they were ten pounds bigger and curvier like their best friend. The friend weighing 114 pounds wishes she were 10 pounds thinner like her 104-pound friend. The blond woman dyes her hair brunette and the brunette woman dyes her hair blond, thinking that true beauty is the right shade in a bottle. It is perfectly okay to change your hair color, but just know that is all that you are changing.

The tall girl wears flat shoes so that she appears shorter and the short girl wears 5-inch heels so that she can appear taller. The person you envy usually envies someone else who she thinks is much more attractive than she is. When is it okay to accept the body you were born with? When and under what circumstances will this body be good enough for you? How many pounds do you need to lose to get to the core of your real beauty?

What shades of hair are you looking for that will give you the beauty, you so desperately seek?

What's the magic number that will make you perfect? How many pounds do you need to lose to be really gorgeous? Who do you think you need to look like to be beautiful? Why do you think this person is more attractive than you? What's wrong with you the way you are? No matter who you think of as being extraordinarily attractive, there is somebody who won't agree with you. So why not claim yourself as one of the most beautiful women in the world!

The media has detached our souls from our bodies by manipulating our minds into believing that we are split beings. We don't view ourselves as a whole person who is comprised of different parts, but separate entities that operate individually. What this means is that when the media only promote certain modes of physical beauty they are indirectly saying that regardless of our genetic composition or our spiritual path, if we exercise with a particular machine or take certain diet pills we will look like the models in the commercials. So what happens is that when we follow a certain exercise or diet regime and do not get the same results as the people in the commercials, we erroneously believe that something is wrong with us. There is absolutely nothing wrong with us. If two people from different genetic backgrounds consumed the exact same amount of calories and did the same type of exercise their bodies would not look identical. Viewing ourselves as a whole being, gives us the ability to understand that the complexity and uniqueness of which we were created cannot and should not be duplicated like clones.

Nudity in American is associated with pornography and eroticism, not with being a sexual, sensuous human being. When only certain types of bodies are validated as worthy of being seen in the media, this is one of the first steps in how we begin to disassociate our minds from our bodies. Psychologically, we don't feel validated as worthy human beings in society unless our image of ourselves is projected into our social reality. Therefore many of the eating disorders such as Anorexia and Bulimia are actually a distorted way of the victim attempting to physically and psychologically exist within their world. When we don't see people like ourselves being praised and admired, we begin to believe that we are unimportant and do not matter. Even when full-figured women who are not thin are showcased in the media; advertisers preface their appearance as being abnormal, using labels such as plus size, queen size and full-figured. They let you know that anyone who is not thin is a deviation from the norm. Many women find it difficult to like themselves when they see weight-loss ads that say, "I used to be a size fourteen, but now I wear a size six." Many normal, beautiful, healthy women wear a size fourteen.

The media disconnects us from our bodies by displaying only certain physical body shapes and sizes. This tells us that if our bodies are not similar in size and shape to the Victoria Secret models or the bikini clad actresses on screen, then our bodies should be kept hidden from others. What happens is that not only do we hide our bodies from others, we hide our bodies from ourselves.

As the nude body that we take glimpses of in the mirror does not look like the ones that we have been exposed to in the media, therefore we believe that the pudgy stomach pouch, stretch marks and cellulite are our personal imperfections, instead of human characteristics of a perfect body. For example, the knots and rings in a beautiful piece of wood are not a flaw of nature, on the contrary, it gives the wood its uniqueness and character.

Your body is not separate from your thoughts. It is not a shoe that comes off at the end of the day. Your body is not a seasonal item that you can put away until it comes back in style. Joyfully owning your physical body is one of the first steps to getting in tune with who you are. It is difficult to love yourself at a spiritual and psychological level, when you are alienated from the most rudimentary element of your being. How can you love the invisible part of your being, when you are repulsed by what you can touch, feel and see on a daily basis? One of the most important things that you can do for your confidence and self-esteem is to stop comparing yourself with people on television's sitcoms, big screen movies and fashion magazines. Look at the people in your community, at the grocery store, malls, schools and doctor's office. These are the lovely people who make the world go round. These are people who have not been airbrushed and their image is not projected from an angle of a camera. Don't *even* compare yourself to them. Just acknowledge the variety of beauty in the world.

Developing a healthy body-image can be achieved by practicing the following nine tips.

1. When you select clothing, make sure that it looks nice on your body. Don't try to imitate your friends or the models in magazines, purchase what looks good on you. The color should compliment your skin tone; the overall fit should be classy and neat. Look your age, not like an insecure woman trying to hold on to her youth. Confidence and self-love are the cornerstones of true beauty. You are not dressing for the body you plan to have in the future. You are not buying clothes for the body you had in the past. Buy your clothes to adorn your beautiful body as it is at this moment.

2. Make sure that you stare at your nude body daily. I don't mean with your bath towel wrapped around you. Look at yourself the way you came into this world. Regardless of what you see, affirm that this is your body and that it

deserves your respect. Look at your body and admit that this is you. One of the reasons that we disassociate ourselves from our bodies is because we avoid mentally connecting with it without clothing, which camouflages and distorts the images of ourselves. If you begin to stare at your naked body on a daily basis, you will be more motivated to take better care of yourself, because at some point you will recognize that your physical body is indeed connected to you.

3. Make a commitment to yourself to stop criticizing your body. No more fat jokes, no more put downs about how dumb you are. There will be zero tolerance of wishing you had someone else's body. You are declaring from this moment forth, that you accept the body that God has blessed you with. Secondly, don't be receptive to anyone else's criticism of your body. Politely tell them that if your body is good enough for God, it is good enough for you.

4. Connect with your body by caressing and nurturing it lovingly like you would the body of a newborn child. Oil your body with slow, long strokes. Take the time to gently massage between your toes. If you use talc or cornstarch sprinkle it slowly on your body and rub it in as if you care. Hum a tune or listen to some soft music while you season your body, as if you are preparing a holiday meal. Lovingly take care of your body.

5. Find at minimum five characteristics that you like about your body. Don't forget things such as your teeth, smile, ears, hairline, navel, toes, and finger nails and so on. Most women centralize their physical beauty in the areas of their thighs, breasts, stomach and buttocks. The purpose of this exercise is to replace negative thoughts about your body with positive thoughts about your body.

6. Absorb non-erotic touch such as hugging your child, shaking a person's hand, or holding hands in a spiritual setting. Realize that your body is not merely validated through sexual or sensuous touch.

7. Pay close attention to your five senses. Your body allows you to interpret and enjoy the world. Eat slowly and really taste your food. See if you can detect the different spices sprinkled in a new recipe. Listen to music; determine what instruments were used and how the words apply to your life. Don't take your body for granted and the wonderful ways that it allows you to interpret and take pleasure in the world.

8. Stop comparing your body to anyone else's. Even though most people are not willing to admit this, they irrationally believe that if they had a perfect body their lives would be perfect. They believe that people with perfect bodies have a better sex life, their food taste better, and that people in general like them more. Halle Barry, Elizabeth Taylor and Christie Brinkley have all been married more than once. Being physically attractive is not the be all or end all, it doesn't make you either better or less than anyone else. Every person is physically attractive depending on who is making the judgment.

9. Find an activity that you can practice in the nude such as yoga or meditation. Spend time alone in your most natural state of being. Initially, this may be difficult. Our society associates nudity with eroticism or pornography. The unclad body is celebrated in art sculptures. Declare your body a vision of loveliness created by God.

10. Find a physical activity that you enjoy such as playing tennis, baseball, basketball and so forth. Enroll in a jazz, ballet, or tap dance class. Learn to use your hands in a craft such as crocheting, knitting, painting or sculpting. Construct a connection with your body and your mind by pouring yourself into an activity that requires the use of both.

CHAPTER 11

▼

WHO ARE YOU WHEN NO ONE IS LOOKING?

Take off your Cloaks

The 13th century meaning of the word *cloak* is "a loose fitting garment or something that envelops or conceals." In this book, the word cloak refers to your external self-constructed identity covers that hide your true self and that have been sanctioned and made conventional by society. The true self has been conditioned by society to dress, act and think in certain ways and to have certain beliefs and ideologies. These cloaks form the visible outer self that has been socialized to adapt to your physical environment. You began developing your cloaks the moment you were identified as a girl or a boy inside of your mommy's belly. Your parents gave you a name that is rich with known or unknown cultural beliefs and has an energy attached to its vibration when uttered. Your name has a subliminal effect on other people based on their race, ethnicity, age, background, political views and income level. Before you become aware of your own existence, society begins cloaking your self-perceptions.

Maybe your natural inclination was to pick up your food with your hands, but your parents taught you to eat with utensils. You learned to say "please," "thank you" and "I am sorry," whether you genuinely meant it or not. Your cloaks are a patchwork of images, words, deeds, and norms sewn together to give you an appearance of fitting in with other people. The cloaks you wear are so dense and obfuscating, that if you ever took them off, you would not recognize yourself.

The naked people are the ones who make other people uncomfortable because their cloaks are missing. The winds of their raw authenticity and truth, force others to hold on tighter to their cloaks. They express ideas that you have been taught to suppress. Their nakedness makes you feel uncomfortable because it is not airbrushed, censored or molded by society's rules and illusions of truth. Many people feel warm, protected and nurtured by their cloaks and pity those who stand alone naked in the cold. The people wearing their cloaks chastise and pity nakedness because they fear their own vulnerability which, when exposed, might not always be a pretty sight.

Everyone wears some cloaks. What's most important is knowing when and where to take them off. What matters is knowing when to reveal your nakedness. You don't know who you are until you have seen yourself naked. In the following sections, you are being asked to take off your cloaks, layer by layer. Who do you find under your socially constructed self? Is this the person you really want to be? Is she scared and alone? What does she look like? You *can* change her by changing how you think about yourself.

Answer the following questions from your heart. Let the answers flow from your soul, not your ego. Take your time answering these questions to exfoliate each layer of your social being to reveal your real, authentic underlying beauty.

Take off Your Political Cloak

1. List 10 reasons why you vote or do not vote for a particular party.

_____

_____

_____

2. What were your parent's political views? Write some of their remarks about politics and candidates in general.

_____

_____

_____

3. How do the majority of your friends and family feel about politics?

_____

_____

_____

4. Have you ever conducted research or learned about governmental power structures?

_____

_____

_____

5. Have you ever reserved sharing your political views because you felt that it would cause others not to like you? If so why did you feel this way?

_____

_____

_____

6. If you were a political leader what are the 3 most important social factors that you would change?

_____

_____

_____

7. Who do you think would be the perfect political leader and why? What do you think are the most important characteristics of a good leader?

_____

_____

_____

8. If given an opportunity would you become a political leader?

_____

_____

_____

Take of Your Religious Cloak

1. In western society divinity and the ultimate good is associated with a male God. Do you think that the patriarchal view of male power, authority and human perfection should in the slightest way affect how women feel about themselves?

_____

_____

_____

2. The Biblical story of Adam and Eve portrays Eve as being responsible for the downfall of humanity. Do you think that this story affects how little girls think of women?

_____

_____

_____

3. Were you required to go to church on Sundays as a child? In what ways do you think your upbringing has shaped your beliefs about traditional religion?

_____

_____

_____

4. How did you learn about God?

_____

_____

_____

5. What were your parent's views about God?

_____

_____

_____

6. How do your friends and family describe and feel about God?

_____

_____

_____

7. Do you think of God differently in private than you do when you are around other people?

_____

_____

_____

8. What do you imagine God to look like and why?

_____

_____

_____

Take off your Body Image Cloak

1. List 10 of the most beautiful women in the world and why you think they are beautiful.

_____
_____
_____

2. How did your mother or other significant women in your family feel about their bodies? List some of the comments that they would make about their own and other women's bodies.

_____
_____
_____

3. What are some the comments that your father or other significant men in your life would make about the female body? Include comments about you, your mother and sister, if applicable. How did these comments make you feel?

_____
_____
_____

4. If you could have the body of any woman in the world whose would it be and why?

_____
_____
_____

5. If you were a man what would you find most attractive about women and why?

_____
_____
_____

6. Stand nude in front of a full-length mirror. How do you feel about your body?

_____
_____
_____

7. Who was the first person who ever told you that you were attractive? How old were you? What was that person like?

_____

_____

_____

8. Describe three times in your life when you felt stunningly attractive and beautiful. What were you wearing? What else was going on in your life at this time?

_____

_____

_____

9. Describe three times in your life when you felt unattractive? What were you wearing? What else was going on in your life at this time?

_____

_____

_____

Take off your Relationship Cloak

1. What type of relationship did your parents and other significant family members share while you were growing up? Did they appear happy? Was infidelity involved? Do you want a relationship like your parents? Why or why not?

_____

_____

_____

2. Do you feel like it is a man's responsibility to financially support a woman? Why or why not? Who taught you to think either way? What did they say?

_____

_____

_____

3. What did your mother and other significant women in your family tell you about men in general?

_____

_____

_____

4. Do you believe that men are biologically designed to be sexually unfaithful in committed relationships?

_____

_____

_____

5. List your favorite three movies about male and female relationships. What are your favorite lines from the movie? What is it that you like about the characters' relationships in these movies?

_____

_____

_____

6. What are the physical, financial and personality traits of the perfect man for you? Do you think that you would be the perfect woman for him? Why or why not?

_____

_____

_____

7. Have you ever had sex with a man in another committed relationship? How did this make you feel about yourself and the other woman?

_____

_____

_____

8. What did your father, brothers or other significant men tell you about men and how they feel about relationships?

_____

_____

_____

Take off your Professional Cloak

1. Did your parents or other significant people in your life encourage you to pursue your dreams when you were a child?

_____

_____

_____

2. Did your parents or other significant people in your life tell you that you are smart or dumb? List specific comments made about your intelligence while growing up.

_____

_____

_____

3. Are you happy in your current job or career? Why or Why not?

_____

_____

_____

4. Are you satisfied with your level of income? Why or Why not?

_____

_____

_____

5. What specifically did your parents or significant other tell you about money?

_____

_____

_____

6. In your heart, do you believe that you could have been anything that you wanted to be? Why or why not?

_____

_____

_____

7. What is your personal definition of success and wealth?

_____

_____

_____

8. Are you currently living the life of your dreams? Why or why not?

_____

_____

_____

9. How did you choose your current job or career?

_____

_____

_____

978-0-595-46022-9
0-595-46022-4